THE TRAGEDY OF DORIAN GRAY

THE TRAGEDY OF DORIAN GRAY

ROSS DINWIDDY

DARE DEVIL

The Tragedy of Dorian Gray

First published in 2020 by Dare Devil

This edition published 2021 by Dare Devil

ISBN 978-0-9926445-5-0

blue
devil
productions

www.bluedeviltheatre.co.uk

The *Tragedy of Dorian Gray* premiered at The Drayton Arms Theatre, South Kensington, London on 19th October 2021, with the following cast.

Maximus Polling as DORIAN GRAY
Jordan Louis as HARRY WOTTON
Chloe Orrock as SYBIL VANE
Christopher Sherwood as BASIL HALLWARD
Heather Alexander as MAVIS RUXTON
Conor Litten as ALAN CAMPBELL

Directed by Ross Dinwiddy
Produced by Rich Bright

Previews of **The Tragedy of Dorian Gray** were staged at The Rialto Theatre, Brighton beginning on 28th May 2021 with the following cast.

Maximus Polling as DORIAN GRAY
Kace Monney as HARRY WOTTON
Tara Clark as SYBIL VANE
Christopher Sherwood as BASIL HALLWARD
Heather Alexander as MAVIS RUXTON
Conor Litten as ALAN CAMPBELL

A filmed version of this production was made with Tom Taplin in the role of Alan Campbell.

Directed by Ross Dinwiddy
Produced by Rich Bright

Blue Devil Productions

THE TRAGEDY OF DORIAN GRAY

A PLAY IN 5 ACTS

ACT 1 – SCENE 1
AN ART GALLERY
LONDON – 1965

There is a smoky haze in the air.

To the rear of stage right, there is a large, wooden easel set with a poster for an exhibition, 'The Helix Gallery, Mayfair. BASIL HALLWARD: ART. 13th February – 9th April 1965. The Male Form in Abstract Time and Space.'

To the front of stage left, there is a black bench.

We hear the sound of a drinks reception party in full swing – chatter, the clink of glasses etc. A distinctly 1960s swing jazz plays softly.

MAVIS RUXTON (40s, wearing high 1960s fashion) enters. She carries a glass of wine and an exhibition pamphlet. She looks around at the people present (theatre audience) with subtle, inspecting interest. She finds her position at centre stage and continues to examine the gathering from her vantage point.

ALAN CAMPBELL (Late 20s, wearing glasses, a tweed jacket & knitted bow tie) enters. He carries a glass of wine and an exhibition pamphlet.

As Alan passes Mavis, she looks him up and down inquisitively.

Alan makes his way to his position at stage right.

BASIL HALLWARD (Early 30s, wearing three-button suit, white turtleneck and a Breton cap) enters. He carries a glass of wine and an exhibition pamphlet.

As Basil passes Mavis, she looks him up and down inquisitively.

Basil makes his way to stage left and sits on the bench.

HARRY WOTTON (Early 30s, sharply dressed in a midnight blue DJ & diamond cut bow tie) enters. He too carries a glass of wine and an exhibition pamphlet. He joins Mavis at centre stage, stands to her left and the two begin to chat.

Alan reads his exhibition pamphlet and sips his wine.

Basil sips his wine too. He looks glum and somewhat irritated.

Mavis and Harry are now deep in conversation, but looking out over the audience; surveying the room.

MAVIS The exhibition is a sensation, of course.

HARRY Of course. Have you seen any of the paintings yet?

MAVIS No. *(Beat)* I'm talking about the turn out for this shindig. Look at this crowd. The place is simply crawling with scoops and exclusives.

HARRY *(Still surveying the room)* Oh yes, there's no shortage of mouth-watering gossip simmering away here tonight, Mavis. Should keep your column worth reading for the next fortnight. *(Alan catches his eye)* Who's that chap over there?

MAVIS Well done. He is a person of interest. Come on, I'll introduce you. See what you make of him.

Mavis escorts Harry over to Alan Campbell.

MAVIS *(Kisses Alan on both cheeks)* Alan Campbell, I'd like you to meet Harry Wotton. My paper once described him as 'Svengali with an office on the King's Road.' – I'm only telling you that because I know how much it irritates him.

ALAN *(Taking off his glasses and shaking Harry's hand)* Good to meet you, Mr Wotton.

HARRY *(To Alan, but throwing Mavis an annoyed sideways glance)* Just Harry, please.

MAVIS You'll be seeing a lot more of Alan soon.

HARRY Will I now?

MAVIS Yes, the BBC is about to announce a major new series – 'Life Lab'. Alan here will be the brilliant, new voice of science for the masses. I'm doing a big write-up on him for next Sunday. He's going to be our centre spread.

ALAN I've been very lucky. I put it all down to my book doing so well. Everything's happened so fast.

MAVIS I worked my way up the hard, slow way. I was William Hickey for 3 years. I'd kill to be on the telly.

HARRY I'm certain Alan's picture on the back of the dust jacket helped most.

ALAN *(Slightly confused)* Excuse me?

HARRY It's just that I notice your brilliant new voice will be heard on the television, not the radio. You're very easy on the eye, Alan.

Alan drops his head, suddenly self-conscious.

ALAN I don't know about…

MAVIS Oh, you must take no notice of Harry. I think he gets his kicks from embarrassing people.

HARRY I bet all the ugly, old professors are just dripping with jealousy. I've never had the slightest interest in test tubes and Bunsen burners, but I'll be an avid viewer.

Harry's attention drifts, he looks across at Basil, who is still sitting on the bench.

ALAN *(Awkwardly)* Thank you, I think.

HARRY Now if you'll excuse me, I must go and have a few words with the artist himself. He looks as if he needs to be consoled on his success.

Harry leaves Mavis and Alan chatting and strolls over to Basil Hallward.

HARRY *(Sits down on the bench next to Basil, but continues to look around the room)* You look miserable, Basil. Why? Tonight's a big, juicy triumph and it's all down to you and your talent.

BASIL You know I hate this sort of thing, Harry. I can't schmooze with these kind of people. And then there was that article in the Express this morning; the bastards called my art 'perverted and degenerate'. *(Glancing round)* Everyone's talking about it.

HARRY Don't worry. Without all the shallow, moral indignation, you'd have half this turnout.

BASIL I've not done all this to have my work gawped at like exhibits in a sideshow.

HARRY Embrace it, Basil. Some dreary millionaire can now purchase an air of danger and sophistication with one of your paintings. Be glad, feel benevolent and for God sake up your prices before people find something else to be scandalised about.

BASIL That's an interesting way of looking at it. Cynical and despicable, but interesting all the same.

HARRY Thank you. Now, if you can't mingle, go and stand somewhere conspicuous and look like an unapproachable, angry young man. You'll certainly be able to manage that. And it'll do just as much good for your reputation, not to mention your sales, as any amount of schmoozing.

SYBIL VANE (Early 30s, wearing a high 1960s fashion, op-art shift dress) enters. She is holding a glass of wine and a pamphlet. She glances around and sips her wine.

BASIL I've really no idea why we're friends, Harry.

HARRY Nor do I. *(Spotting Sybil – his eyes fix on*

her) It's another of life's sweet mysteries. *(Getting to his feet)* Now I must go and discover a few things about the other talk-of-the-town.

Harry moves swiftly away from Basil. He joins Sybil near centre stage.

Mavis and Alan are close by still chatting.

HARRY Sybil, my darling. It's lovely to see you back in London.

SYBIL Harry. It's lovely to be back.

HARRY And of course, congratulations.

SYBIL *(Clinking glasses with Harry)* Thank you.

HARRY So Hollywood hasn't completely stolen you from us, *(Beat)* yet.

SYBIL Not at all. I've been offered a role at the Royal Court that was simply made for me. So, naturally, I'm considering it very seriously and that would keep me in town for well over a year.

Mavis is now clearly eavesdropping.

HARRY The Court. Kept for over a year. Sounds as if you're talking about a sentence. But isn't it the Oscar that's supposed to be a golden shackle? You know, a strong leash to keep your beauty, your talent where it can be exploited to the full?

SYBIL *(Pulling an unamused face)* What's the view like from all the way up there, Harry?

HARRY Oh, please don't imagine I'm being condescending. A restraint that luxurious, that exclusive would be thrilling to submit to.

SYBIL Well, I'm still deciding if I want to wear the Oscar around my neck or not. We'll see.

HARRY Don't ponder for too long, Sybil. How old are you now?

SYBIL *(Narrows her eyes, then...)* Thirty one.

HARRY Thirty one – then I'd get cracking if I were you. The people in the stalls and the gallery can wait a little, the close-up cannot.

Harry gently strokes his finger on the skin near the corner of Sybil's right eye.

Sybil yanks her face away from Harry's touch.

SYBIL Harry, you really are the most…

MAVIS *(Pulling away from Alan and butting in)* Sybil, darling, it's a proper tonic to see you here. And alone too. I knew that scurrilous story in all the rags couldn't possibly be true.

SYBIL Which scurrilous story is that, Mavis?

MAVIS The one about you secretly marrying a mere child you hardly know, of course.

Alan looks awkward, he glances around then exits.

Harry notices and watches him go.

SYBIL Oh, that. I can't say I've read all the rags but I did see it in the one you work for.

MAVIS But not written by me, my love. Not by me. So, no truth in it then?

SYBIL It's all quite untrue. *(Beat)* I've known Dorian Gray for well over 6 months and he's 21, so hardly a child.

HARRY *(Looking away, almost to himself)* Dorian Gray, never heard of him.

MAVIS *(Looking flabbergasted, yet excited)* Are you telling me that you are… you did… you..?

HARRY *(Interrupting)* I see that double congratulations are in order, then. Presumably you'll keep Sybil Vane. 'Starring Mrs Sybil Gray' sounds so… well, grey.

MAVIS Is this Dorian Gray here tonight? I must meet him.

HARRY *(Almost to himself again and glancing around)* So must I.

Sybil takes a deep breath, then…

SYBIL Yes, he's here somewhere. *(Beat)* He was looking at the pictures.

MAVIS Perhaps we should all go and have a shufti. *(Heading for the exit – stage left)* That way, we're bound to find Mr Gray.

Harry follows Mavis to the exit stage left.

After a moment, an apprehensive Sybil follows too.

As they leave, DORIAN GRAY (Early 20s, wearing a tonic, single-breasted suit, narrow burgundy tie and Chelsea boots) enters stage right looking around languidly as he does so. He carries a wine glass with very little wine in it and a pamphlet. When Dorian reaches centre stage, he glances at Basil, who is still sitting on the bench.

DORIAN *(To Basil, casually)* They're very good.

BASIL *(Not really paying Dorian any attention)* Excuse me.

DORIAN *(Draining his glass as he moves closer to Basil)* The paintings, they're very good.

BASIL 'Good' is not the word they're using to describe them in the papers.

DORIAN That sort of thing doesn't interest me. I like them.

Basil turns and looks up at Dorian. He suddenly seems transfixed by the young man's face.

DORIAN I would think that the artist finds that kind of attention annoying, hurtful even.

BASIL *(Still studying Dorian's face)* What makes you say that?

DORIAN I don't think he's done any of this to shock

7

or cause a scandal. There's a sensitivity to the paintings. With them, he's telling us stuff that's very private. There are things he needs to express about himself, but he'll only confide in those who can be bothered to look, really look. In a way, I think these pictures show more of this man, Basil Hallward, than they do of the young men in them – and they do reveal a lot.

BASIL *(Laughing and getting to his feet)* Look, I think I should tell you, I am Basil Hallward.

DORIAN *(Embarrassed)* Oh. I'm very sorry. I really hope I haven't made a fool of myself, Mr Hallward.

BASIL Basil, please. And no, you haven't made a fool of yourself. In fact, I very much appreciate what you've said about me and my work. *(Smiles warmly)* Right, you have my name, may I ask yours?

DORIAN Dorian. Dorian Gray.

BASIL I don't suppose you'd sit for me, Dorian?

DORIAN Sit?

BASIL So that I can paint you. I'd very much like to.

DORIAN *(Frowning)* Umm...

BASIL Please say you will.

DORIAN I've never modelled or anything like that. I really don't know.

BASIL Please.

DORIAN *(Gathering his thoughts)* Mr Hallw... Basil, having seen your work, I'm a little intimidated by the idea, to be perfectly honest with you.

BASIL Intimidated, I see. But you shouldn't be. I'd never ask you to do anything you're not comfortable with. Anyway, it's just a portrait I'm after. You see, I feel a compelling need to capture your face at this precise instant in your life. Capture you.

DORIAN *(Self-consciously touching his cheek)* I'm flattered, really I am. Will you let me think about it? Not for long. *(Beat)* Perhaps I can let you know sometime tomorrow?

BASIL Yes. Yes, of course… *(Noticing that Dorian's wine glass is empty)* Now, let me get you a drink, another glass of wine. There's some good stuff tucked away, just for me and my friends.

Dorian smiles and hands Basil his glass

ACT 1 – SCENE 2
A BEDROOM IN SYBIL'S HOUSE NEAR REGENT'S PARK

SYBIL, dressed only in her petticoat/slip, sits at her dressing table. She is removing her makeup and false eyelashes etc. On the dressing there is a hand mirror, a hairbrush, perfume atomiser and a jar of cold cream. There is also a small tray with a bottle of Dimple Haig whisky, and 2 glasses.

DORIAN lies on the bed in his suit trousers and shirt (as previous scene but without shoes, the jacket and tie). He is reading a thick script, 'The Female Factory', the pages are held together with a strong bulldog clip.

Sybil studies her face in the hand mirror, paying particular attention to the skin around her eyes.

SYBIL Was it all too awful for you, Dorian?

DORIAN *(Not looking up from the script)* Not in the slightest. In fact, I enjoyed this evening very much.

SYBIL Really?

DORIAN Really.

SYBIL You certainly kept a low profile.

DORIAN Not intentionally. People weren't there to see me. You, on the other hand…

SYBIL Well, a pair of ravenous blood hounds called

Harry Wotton and Mavis Ruxton are now on your scent and even they couldn't track you down. *(Chuckles)* They'll be livid and simply seething with frustration. *(More seriously)* Mind you, that'll make both of them twice as interested, twice as determined.

DORIAN OK, I'll brace myself. *(Beat)* Are they very similar types?

SYBIL No. The only thing they really have in common is that I wouldn't trust either of them in an empty shop. *(Starting to brush her hair)* So, what was it about tonight that you enjoyed so much?

DORIAN Lots of things. The paintings were brilliant *(Beat)* and I had a very interesting conversation with the artist, Basil Hallward himself.

Sybil stops brushing her hair and turns to face Dorian, who is still reading the script.

SYBIL Well, that does surprise me.

DORIAN It was easy, he made me feel very relaxed, comfortable. I liked him immediately.

SYBIL Not so much that you were happy to talk to him, more that he condescended to talk to you. Most people find *dear* Basil utterly dismissive.

DORIAN Not me – quite the opposite. He even wants to paint me.

SYBIL Paint you? *(Standing)* I see. *(Looks at Dorian inquisitively for a moment, then…)* Don't tell me you're actually considering it.

DORIAN That's exactly what I am doing.

SYBIL *(Sternly)* Are you? His paintings are rather… *(Raising her eyebrows)* Well, I'd call them…

DORIAN *(Cutting in)* This wouldn't be like his usual stuff. He's just talking about a portrait.

SYBIL A portrait… *(Thoughtfully)* A portrait of you by Basil Hallward. *(She suddenly seems very pleased)*

11

Oh, that's totally different. In which case, I really do hope you're going to say 'yes'.

DORIAN I said I'd sleep on it, but I think I've already made my mind up. I'll do it.

SYBIL Oh, that's fantastic. Tell him I'll want to buy it. He mustn't even entertain the idea of selling it to anyone else.

DORIAN OK, I'll tell him. *(Closes the script, gets up and goes over to Sybil)* I think this is very good. *(Shakes the script)*

SYBIL *(Taking the script)* 'The Female Factory' a brand new play by Jack Chadwick; and it's all mine if I want it. *(Drops the script on the dressing table)* I'd even get to use my own accent for once.

Sybil then pours whisky into two tumblers. As she does so…

SYBIL Anyway, whoever ends up starring in it, it's going to be something really special – I'm certain of that.

Sybil gives a glass to Dorian.

DORIAN Cheers.

SYBIL Cheers. *(Beat)* I've been thinking, if we were to stay in London, there might even be a chance I'll get proper access to Hetty.

DORIAN Makes sense.

SYBIL Andrew's not an unreasonable man… *(through gritted teeth)* for the most part. Since the divorce, he's at least *attempted* to be civilised.

Sybil takes a large swig of the whisky.

SYBIL I've been clean for over a year now and I'm more confident than ever I'm going to stay that way. Judging by the party tonight, cocaine is certainly coming back into fashion. And, do you know? I wasn't even tempted. *(Beat)* I've also got this under control now, *(She lifts her glass of whisky)* haven't I?

DORIAN *(Reassuringly, touching Sybil gently on her arm.)* Yes… yes you have.

SYBIL It's got to be worth me at least thinking about shared custody, don't you think?

DORIAN Of course, we should work towards that. It has to be possible now. *(Beat)* That old nursery at the top of the house could be converted into the most amazing room for her.

SYBIL It's an attic, Dorian. And she's only four.

DORIAN When she's a bit older then. And it's a huge attic, any kid would love it. I know I would have.

SYBIL *(With a loving smile)* That reminds me, I found this up there the other day.

Sybil reaches under the dressing table and produces an old brass and walnut metronome.

SYBIL *(Rubbing a bit of dust off the metronome.)* It's showing its age, but I think it's rather beautiful.

She hands it to Dorian.

SYBIL I thought you might like it.

DORIAN Like it? *(Beat, smiles)* I love it. I'll use it always, I promise.

Dorian wanders back to the bed and sits, his attention fixed on the metronome.

DORIAN I'll put it to work first thing tomorrow. *(Puts down the metronome and looks up at Sybil)* My new song.

Sybil looks at Dorian for a moment, thoughtfully. Her expression becomes one of contentment and joy. She turns and picks up the script from the dressing table.

SYBIL I've hardly seen Hetty this last six months. If I don't look out, she'll be all grown-up and I'll have missed the lot. Hetty, you and meaningful work like this *(She shakes the script as she walks over to Dorian, then drops it onto the bed)* Think what life could be like. *(Beat)* Hollywood can go hang… for now at any rate. I'm going to do it; the play and everything else. Are you ready to be a stepfather?

DORIAN I think so.

SYBIL *(Sitting down on the bed)* And more immediately, are you ready for the world to know you're my husband?

DORIAN More than ready.

SYBIL Take a deep breath – the pair of us are going to be spread-eagled in the press over the next few days. Mavis and co will see to that. *(She gently strokes Dorian's face)* All their appetites will be whetted by you – fresh meat.

DORIAN We knew it was coming. I'm glad all the petty subterfuge can end. I'm curious to see what this fame thing is like.

Sybil looks into Dorian's eyes for a moment, then...

SYBIL You're not particularly interested in fame, are you, Dorian?

DORIAN *(With a small, supressed laugh)* I've never really thought about it.

SYBIL Really? Not even with your band? Don't you dream of being a pin-up for hordes of salivating, teenage girls?

DORIAN You know it's all about the music for me.

They kiss.

SYBIL *(Sybil holds eye-contact with Dorian)* Well, I hope you don't mind being my sexy pin-up. Now, where are we gonna hang this painting?

They kiss again and as they fall back onto the bed.

ACT 2 – SCENE 1
BASIL'S STUDIO
IN CHELSEA

There is a large wooden easel towards the front of stage right. On this is a large canvas but the painting faces away from the audience, obscuring the picture. Next to this is a small table with oil paint tubes, jars, brushes etc.

There is a small stool towards the front of stage left.

BASIL is dressed in a well-used French workman's jacket which is splattered with paint. He sits on a bench towards the rear of the stage. Next to him on the bench is an equally well-used artists palette and a bundle of brushes. He begins to examine the tip of a very fine brush from the bundle.

HARRY enters from stage left, dressed in a sharp suit and a dark Crombie overcoat.

BASIL *(Looking up)* Harry, I wasn't expecting you.

HARRY I was just passing and thought – I haven't seen Basil for over two months, why not pop in and find out why he's been hiding.

BASIL Did you? *(Eyes Harry suspiciously)* Well, whilst it's lovely to see you, I am rather busy today and...

HARRY Are you? Busy with what... *(Glancing round)* and who?

Harry spots the painting and strides over to take a look.

BASIL *(Springing to his feet)* Please don't look at that, it's not finished.

Harry looks anyway. He seems transfixed.

HARRY Remarkable. It's utterly unlike your usual work. Such a different style. *(Pause)* I love it. In fact, if I weren't standing here right now, I wouldn't even believe you really were the artist.

BASIL *(Bitterly)* Thank you very much.

HARRY It's curious, the subject looks very familiar, very familiar indeed; yet I'm quite certain I've never met this gorgeous young man.

BASIL If I've anything to do with it, you never will.

HARRY *(Turning back to Basil)* Don't be childish. Who is he? Where'd he come from?

BASIL I don't know if I want to tell you his name. I met him at the opening of my exhibition. He struck up a conversation with me. *(Beat)* But I'd actually first seen him over an hour earlier and I'd been avoiding him.

HARRY Avoiding him, why on earth would you want to avoid him?

BASIL I was on my own, finding most people there repellent. So far, so typical. Then, suddenly, here was somebody that I was actually drawn to; but drawn to with such force that it terrified me. You can call it cowardice if you like, but I quickly became convinced that we should never meet. That I should under no circumstances give in to my passionate desire to paint him. Perhaps I was frightened he'd overwhelm me and my art. *(Beat)* No, I was confident that he would.

HARRY How very interesting. And has he?

BASIL There's the evidence. *(He flicks the back of his hand in the direction of the painting)* It's utterly unlike anything I've ever done, or so I'm told.

HARRY *(Narrowing his eyes)* So, your efforts to avoid him clearly failed.

BASIL I was attempting to be invisible, when an unfamiliar voice spoke to me. I looked round and there was Dorian Gray.

HARRY *(Triumphant)* Dorian Gray!

Harry moves back to the painting and studies it.

BASIL It felt so inevitable. The next thing I knew, I was begging him to sit for me. I couldn't help myself.

HARRY *(Eyes still fixed on the painting)* And of course this is bound to be the Dorian Gray that the whole of London is desperate to meet. *(Looks back at Basil)* Where is he now?

BASIL *(Reluctantly)* On a break, having a cigarette in the garden.

HARRY He's here now! In which case, if you want to get rid of me, you're going to have to physically throw me out.

Dorian enters stage left. He is dressed only in a plain blue dressing gown. He is unnoticed by Harry and Basil.

BASIL Harry, please, Dorian is completely…

DORIAN Are you two talking about me?

Harry and Basil look round.

Harry dashes over and shakes Dorian warmly by the hand.

Basil pushes his fingers through his hair. He looks very put out and irritated.

HARRY Mr Gray, it's a pleasure to meet you at last. I can't tell you how I've been looking forward to seeing you in the flesh.

DORIAN Oh, call me Dorian, please.

BASIL This is Harry, an old friend. And please, don't listen to a word he has to say.

DORIAN Harry. Harry Wotton?

HARRY That's right.

DORIAN *(With a small laugh)* It's good to meet you too. I've heard a lot about you.

HARRY And all of it shocking, I hope. So you're the young prince who married queen Sybil Vane. I understand you're a burgeoning star of popular music.

DORIAN Not a star, but I was in a band.

HARRY Was?

DORIAN We broke up, but I'm going to form another.

HARRY And then you'll be a star?

DORIAN Oh, I hope not.

HARRY So your driving ambition for this new band is for it to be a failure? With your looks, you have to be a star, need to be a star. Anyway, the decision shouldn't be yours to make.

DORIAN Shouldn't it? *(Beat)* I think I'm starting to understand why people say the things they do about you, Harry.

BASIL *(Impatient. picking up his palette and brush)* We do need to get on, Dorian. Harry is just leaving.

DORIAN OK, Basil. Excuse me, Harry.

Dorian goes over to the stool, sits down and adopts a pose for the painting.

Basil stands at the easel and studies the painting.

BASIL *(Almost to himself, concentrating)* There's not much left to do. Just a few details in the eyes.

Harry makes no attempt to leave. He sits down on the bench, his eyes fixed on Dorian.

HARRY I've seen quite a number of photographs of you in the press over the last few months, but those grainy snaps just don't do you justice.

BASIL Harry, I thought you said you had an important appointment and had to go. You know, that thing at three o'clock on the other side of town. It does sound as if you have to be there.

HARRY I've said nothing of the sort, Basil. In fact, I don't know what you're talking about.

DORIAN Let Harry stay, Basil. Please.

BASIL *(Reluctantly)* If you want him to stay, then of course he can stay.

HARRY So, how are you finding being a married man at the tender age of twenty-one?

DORIAN I don't think I've been happier in my life.

HARRY Oh, how tragic. Your life must have been horrible.

DORIAN Life's been fine – it's just that it's even better now. I'm very much in love with the kindest, brightest, most beautiful and talented actress – Sybil Vane. She is my wife and soon we'll have her daughter to join our happy family. I'm very content.

HARRY Content! What a nasty condition for someone so young. You should be anything but content at your age. Save that hideous limbo for nearer the grave.

DORIAN It's what I want. It's all I want.

HARRY Is it? *(Beat)* You seem determined to throw away your youth, the most valuable and irreplaceable commodity you will ever possess. Extraordinary. And all coupled with this disturbing hunger for the most cloying normality.

BASIL Hold your head a little more to the light, Dorian.

Dorian slightly moves his head.

BASIL Perfect.

HARRY Yet you go looking for this normality in the most abnormal of places – you've married into the acting profession; where youth and all it entails is positively idolised. But, in your case, you have to give it up to get in.

DORIAN I'm not an actor, nor do I want to be one.

HARRY No, your ambitions are in the music industry; which if anything, is even worse.

BASIL I think it's finished.

Dorian rushes over to see the painting.

Harry stands, then follows slowly.

HARRY Now that does do you justice, it's every bit as stunning as you are.

DORIAN It's incredible, Basil. Do I look like that?

HARRY Yes, just like that. It's uncanny and unsettlingly lifelike. *(Turning to Basil)* Where will you display it?

BASIL Absolutely nowhere, this one won't go public.

DORIAN *(With his eyes still fixed on the painting)* Sybil wants to buy it. It'll be just for us.

HARRY Ridiculous! I'll buy it, I'll display it. Whatever Sybil has offered, I'll pay double. I need to see what the world thinks of it and subsequently, what the world will have in store for you both.

BASIL You're a mischievous man, Harry. And by the way, I'd never sell it to you. I don't care how much money you offer. *(Turning to Dorian)* And I don't intend selling it to Sybil either.

DORIAN *(Turning to face Basil with a look of disappointment)* What?

BASIL I'm giving it to you, Dorian, as a gift.

DORIAN Really, Basil?

BASIL Of course. It was yours before I even began work on it. It *is* you.

HARRY But this painting must be seen, seen by as many people as possible! I don't know which of you it would benefit most. Basil, it's a masterpiece – I can see the gushing critical analysis now. But Dorian, everyone will want a part of the beguiling creature it depicts. And that will go on forever, for as long as there are eyes to look at it.

DORIAN I don't know…

HARRY You should know! The painting is now yours. Not Sybil's, not Basil's and you can use it in whatever way you see fit. But you'll need to strike quickly, before you age too much and the real you begins to bitterly disappoint.

Harry's words seem to hit a chord with Dorian. He turns back to the painting and moves in close again, studying it in detail, particularly the face.

DORIAN Yes. It'll always look like this and I won't. Do you think that one day, those eyes will look back and mock me?

HARRY Certainly they'll mock you. Mock you terribly. You have youth you wish to throw away, beauty you wish to hide until it has jaded and musical talent you are hell bent to turn into failure. Yes, in time the young man in the painting will remind you of what you've squandered and he will be merciless in his scorn and his derision. Don't let this exquisite painting bring you nothing but pain and regret as the years pass.

DORIAN *(Breaking away from the painting and turning to Harry)* Stop it, Harry, stop.

Harry examines the distressed look on Dorian's face and develops an amused smile.

HARRY Are you still glad to have met me, Dorian?

DORIAN *(Shaken, but holding eye contact with Harry)* I'm going to need to think about that.

HARRY I see. *(Beat)* Well, now that you've finished here, why don't you contemplate it over a few drinks with me at the Blue Turtle. *(Toying with the lapel of Dorian's dressing gown)* Put your clothes on and I'll call a cab.

Dorian seems to study Harry's eyes for a moment.

DORIAN *(Slowly)* Yes, I think I'd like that. *(Suddenly moving away from Harry)* I've never been to the Blue Turtle.

BASIL *(Hurt and disappointed)* I was going to open a bottle of wine. *(To Harry)* Me and Dorian usually have a drink together at the end of the day.

DORIAN Oh, Basil you should have said. I've agreed to go with Harry now. Why don't you come with us?

BASIL I don't think so.

HARRY *(To Dorian)* You should telephone Sybil and say you'll be late. Explain that you're with me, that should put her mind at rest.

DORIAN *(Amused)* I think I am glad to have met you, Harry. I wonder if I shall always be.

ACT 2 – SCENE 2
THE LIVING ROOM
IN SYBIL'S HOUSE

The painting and easel are still towards the front of stage facing away from the audience, but are now covered up with a sheet.

There are a few open bottles of Champagne positioned about the stage, together with a number of empty glasses.

A get-together is in full swing. There is the sound of merry chatter and the clinking of glasses. 1960s easy listening, light jazz plays softly. The lights are soft and low. There is a smoky haze in the air.

HARRY (in a well-tailored, shark skin suit) and BASIL (in his 3 button suit and Breton cap) are deep in conversation at stage left. They each have a glass of Champagne.

MAVIS (Again in high 60s fashion) and ALAN (Wearing his tweed jacket and knitted bow tie) are at stage right chatting. They too have a glass of Champagne each.

HARRY So the unveiling of the painting isn't going to be as private and intimate as you expected.

BASIL *(Looking around)* Dorian assured me it would be just close friends and family.

HARRY *(Nodding in Mavis's direction)* I notice that 'close friends' now include journalists like Mavis Ruxton and a gaggle of photographers.

BASIL That'll be Sybil's doing. She's always shamelessly courted publicity.

HARRY I'd say publicity has always shamelessly courted her. Anyway, I know Dorian had quite a hand in the guest list, *(Beat)* with a little guidance and encouragement from me.

BASIL *(Wearily)* I see.

HARRY Now, Basil, have you done as I said? No one can be allowed to see the painting until you present it at exactly 8 o'clock. We need to keep them waiting.

BASIL Yes, I've followed your instructions.

Basil and Harry turn and chat silently as our attention moves to…

MAVIS Alan, I hear you're involved in Dustin Hawk's next artistic event.

ALAN Yes, that's right.

DORIAN (In his tonic suit, purple tie and Chelsea boots) enters from stage left.

MAVIS Dustin is so handsome, don't you think?

ALAN *(Avoiding eye contact with Mavis)* Is he?

Dorian greets Harry and Basil warmly as he passes them on his way across the stage.

MAVIS Oh yes, really sexy. And such a rebel.

ALAN *(Clears his throat, nervously)* The event is going to be a real spectacular. Dustin enrolled my help basically because he'd seen me on television…

Alan notices Dorian.

Dorian has reached a bottle of Champagne near Mavis and Alan. He takes a glass and pours himself a drink.

ALAN …We're going to dissolve a whole dead elephant in a massive, specially built, glass tank.

DORIAN *(Turning to join Alan and Mavis)* You're going to dissolve a dead elephant?

MAVIS *(Probing, almost excited)* The poor creature wasn't killed especially for this, was it? Slaughtered in the name of art!

ALAN Oh, no. It was natural causes – old age. He passed away in the new elephant house at London Zoo two weeks ago; just across the park from here *(Points)*. The body's being kept in cold storage until the big day.

DORIAN But how on earth would you even go about dissolving a whole elephant?

ALAN Well, science… biochemistry to be exact. Put simply, we'll use alkaline hydrolysis to strip it to the bone. Then the tank will be drained and refilled with good old sulphuric acid, which will completely dissolve the skeleton. It's all going to be filmed and played back, speeded-up, to Flight Of The Bumblebee.

MAVIS How marvellous! And I've always had a soft spot for a bit of Rimsky Korsakov. *(Something catches her attention)* Wait a moment, David Bailey's chatting with Shrimpton *(beat)* again.

They all look out over the audience, dodging their heads about for a better look.

MAVIS And he's got *that* look in his eye.

Mavis darts off.

MAVIS *(As she goes)* Don't go anywhere, I'll be back.

ALAN *(Moving a little closer to Dorian)* Dorian, would you like to come and see the filming next Wednesday? It's very restricted, but I could certainly get you in.

SYBIL (In a dogtooth mini-dress) enters from stage left. She greats Harry and Basil as she heads for centre stage.

DORIAN It would be just me, I'm afraid. Sybil's busy

all next week.

ALAN Sybil. *(He seems surprised)* Oh, yes, Sybil. No, just you will be fine. Great. I'd like that.

SYBIL *(Addressing the whole room including the theatre audience)* Ladies and gentlemen, ladies and gentlemen, I have a small announcement. I want you all, my dear friends, to be the first to know.

Marvis has returned, she listens at stage left.

SYBIL I've just agreed to do Jack Chadwick's new play, 'The Female Factory', at the Royal Court. Jack is here tonight… *(She glances round)* Somewhere… and I can't wait to start rehearsals.

There is a round of applause from the room.

Dorian steps up and embraces Sybil.

Harry, still at stage left, steps away from Basil and helps himself to more Champagne.

Alan joins Dorian and Sybil, they all chat and settle towards stage right.

Mavis moves in close to Harry, who tops up her glass.

HARRY *(Studying Sybil and Dorian from across the room)* So she rejected Hollywood after all.

MAVIS Not quite. David Lean is in the midst of the most elaborate pre-production for his latest epic. And from what I've heard, Sybil is top of the short list for the female lead. Treading the boards will keep her respectable and her profile high enough until he gets round to final casting. I'd call it a shrewd move.

HARRY *(Not taking his eyes off Sybil and Dorian)* A glorious gamble, all the same.

MAVIS Perhaps, but don't forget, the studio didn't want her for 'Death of a Yellow Bird', they pushed for an established movie star. But the director insisted on the original cast from the London stage and that led all the way to her Oscar triumph.

Harry turns to face Mavis and nods thoughtfully.

MAVIS So should the 'glorious gamble' not pay off… Well, there are whispers that Tony Richardson has his eye on 'The Female Factory' *(She winks)* for more of his black and white, worthy grit. If I know that, there's every chance Sybil knows it too.

Basil walks over to the easel at stage right.

Sybil moves back to centre stage and…

SYBIL *(Again addressing the whole room)* Everyone, everyone! The time has finally arrived. Basil Hallward is ready to unveil his portrait of Dorian!

Harry walks over to Sybil.

HARRY I haven't asked what you think of the painting yet, Sybil.

SYBIL I've not seen it. Basil has been his usual inscrutable self; refusing to let anyone see it until the *grand* unveiling at *exactly* 8 o'clock. *(Rolls her eyes)*

HARRY Oh, we all have to indulge dear old Basil, don't we?

SYBIL Anyway, perhaps it's for the best. All the theatrics has got me so excited.

Harry just smiles.

Basil stands to stage right, next to the easel.

The guests all gather round.

BASIL *(Taking hold of the corner of the sheet that covers the painting)* Ladies and gentlemen, I'd very much like to present 'The Picture of Dorian Gray'.

Basil pulls the sheet off the painting.

There is a stunned silence as everyone edges a little closer to the painting

Harry examines their reaction for a moment then starts to clap his hands. Soon everyone else joins in.

After a few seconds, Mavis pulls her eyes away from the painting and makes straight for Dorian. She takes him by the arm and manoeuvres him to stage left.

They are soon deep in conversation.

Simultaneously, Sybil further approaches the painting as if in a trance, hypnotised by its beauty.

SYBIL Basil, I thought it would be good, great even, but this is extraordinary. I love it. No, more than that, it's the most beautiful thing I've ever seen.

BASIL Besides Dorian himself.

Alan nods slowly, also transfixed by the painting.

SYBIL But it *is* Dorian, they seem to be the same thing. You've captured him perfectly. His spirit, his personality; it's so much more than simply what he looks like. It's the most astonishing achievement.

Harry joins them.

HARRY *(To Sybil)* Even with your splendid 'Female Factory' news, you've got to agree that the night belongs to Dorian and his painting.

SYBIL Of course.

HARRY There just isn't room in the spotlight for the three of you this evening. Isn't it dazzling?

SYBIL Yes, 'dazzling' is the word.

ALAN *(Slowly, a little breathless)* I've never seen oil paint shimmer and glow like that. *(Taking off his glasses and moving in even closer)* It seems to be almost iridescent.

Harry and Basil leave Sybil and Alan chatting about the painting and go over to join Mavis, who is still talking with Dorian.

MAVIS The new play will be a sensation. People often say things like 'finest actress of her generation', but with Sybil, it's true. And she's such a superb story too

– from rags to riches, then spectacularly crashing down to rock bottom. Now soaring back to dizzying heights. Just the sort of thrill ride the public loves.

DORIAN I think I'd call her 'a survivor', not 'a story'.

MAVIS Of course, of course.

HARRY Exactly, Dorian. You know, she was cast as Juliet at Stratford straight out of drama school. She was the same age as you are now, and she was divine. Utterly captivating and divine.

DORIAN I wish I'd seen that.

HARRY Yes, it's a shame they didn't do a school outing or anything like that.

MAVIS Oh she's hardly changed, but there was a certain something about her then. If only you'd painted her, Basil. Imagine the two portraits hanging together now.

BASIL I don't think Sybil would have inspired quite the same style; they'd look odd side by side.

Sybil and Alan exit, still chatting.

HARRY Yes, I can well imagine that.

MAVIS Now, Dorian, I'll get a photographer to take lots of pictures of you next to the painting. I'll do an interview with you; a proper sit down chat tomorrow, and hopefully Basil too.

BASIL I don't think so…

MAVIS Come on, it won't do you any harm to get some good press for a change. At least give me a few provocative quotes to get me started…

Mavis takes Basil by the arm and leads him to the rear of stage right.

Harry watches them go, then looks to Dorian.

HARRY The painting is certainly casting its spell.

DORIAN *(With a serious expression)* Yes. Everyone wants to know *me* now. Act, model, form another band – all of those things, and more, have been suggested tonight. It's just as you predicted.

HARRY Why not crack a smile then? Enjoy this experience. Moments like this don't last long.

DORIAN *(Now with a small smile)* I know, but there'll always be the painting to remind me.

HARRY Yes, the painting is locked in this instant. It will always be as it is tonight.

Mavis and Basil's conversation seems to have ended badly. Mavis exits muttering with irritation.

Basil stands with his arms folded, also muttering, annoyed.

DORIAN *(Now jovially)* If only it were the other way round; that the painting suffered the marks of time and I never changed. That would stop it ever looking back at me with pity and contempt.

HARRY Well, that sounds like the perfect arrangement. But I can't imagine a deal like that coming cheaply. What would you offer up in return?

DORIAN I don't know. *(Beat)* What about my soul? Do you think that would do the trick?

HARRY Your soul should be more than enough. For goodness sake don't bargain away your body too. You're going to need it to reap a lifetime of sensual rewards as you remain forever desirable.

DORIAN *(Chuckling and looking round)* I can't see Sybil anywhere. I want to ask her advice on what to say to Mavis.

HARRY And what not to say. Very wise.

DORIAN Excuse me, Harry.

Dorian exits.

Harry goes to a bottle of Champagne and begins refilling his glass.

Basil walks up behind Harry and eyes him suspiciously for a moment, then...

BASIL Earlier, I overheard some people gossiping that Dorian has secretly signed to a very prominent record label. Do you know anything about that?

HARRY *(Topping up Basil's glass)* Eavesdropping, Basil. I'm surprised at you. It's not true, *(beat)* yet. But useful enough tittle-tattle.

BASIL Something's been set in motion here tonight, Harry. Something we don't fully understand.

HARRY Oh, I understand it. Dorian Gray has become quite a project for me. But it's a project that needs *all* our gifts – your artistry, *(gestures in the direction of the painting)* Sybil's fame, my... *(Beat)* cunning and his beauty. It's going to be the most fabulous and rewarding adventure for us all.

BASIL You think so? *(Beat)* You see, I feel the most dreadful sense of foreboding – that we'll all suffer for what the Gods have given us. Suffer terribly.

ACT 3 – SCENE 1
THE BEDROOM IN SYBIL'S HOUSE
1966

DORIAN is in his blue dressing gown. He sits on the bed reading a book called 'The Vanity of Vane' by Mavis Ruxton.

SYBIL paces the stage, furious. She holds another copy of the book.

On the dressing table (to the front of stage) there is a small, brown bottle of pills. There is also a small tray with a bottle of Dimple Haig whisky and 2 glasses.

SYBIL *(With contempt)* 'The Vanity of Vane' I expect that cow Mavis thought it was a cute title.

DORIAN *(Not looking up from the book)* I'm almost finished.

SYBIL And with the custody hearing on the horizon, the last thing we needed was to have everyone reminded about all this. *(Shakes the book with fury)* I could kill her!

DORIAN Sybil, calm down.

SYBIL Sorry. *(Making for the dressing table)* Christ, I need one of my little helpers.

Sybil flings the book onto the dressing table, picks up the small brown bottle, shakes out a pill, then washes it down with a gulp of Scotch.

Dorian finishes the last page, closes the book and tosses it onto the bed.

DORIAN *(Raising his eyebrows)* Well.

SYBIL Well?

DORIAN Well what?

SYBIL *(Walking back to the bed)* Well, should I sue the two-faced, poisonous bitch?

DORIAN What for?

SYBIL What for! It's a stinking catalogue of libel, with my name *(Picking up Dorian's copy of the book)* and face all over it. Not to mention that the fucking thing is selling like cold pop in a heat wave.

DORIAN *(Standing and taking the book from her)* It's only libel if it's untrue.

SYBIL Whose side are you on?

DORIAN Yours, of course. But look, if Mavis can prove it's true and you go after her, she'll win, you'll lose, and lose badly.

SYBIL It's all an outrageous exaggeration.

DORIAN That's a shame. To be perfectly honest, it's rather turned me on.

Dorian takes Sybil in his arms.

Sybil is calmer now, comforted by Dorian's embrace.

SYBIL Really? What, the thought of me with other men?

DORIAN Yes, and women.

SYBIL *(Playfully)* You're becoming such a bad boy. I do hope it's not my influence.

DORIAN *(Also Playfully)* If only it were. The ideas are there, but I'm not making much practical progress. Now with your help and experience, I could easily become positively wicked, with a little effort.

SYBIL I'm a respectable married woman now.

DORIAN Marriage didn't seem to get in your way before. According to Mavis, my predecessor, the virtuous Andrew, was deeply involved.

SYBIL It was our wild and reckless youth. I'm the all-new, reformed Sybil Vane now.

DORIAN I'll be twenty-two in a few weeks and I've nothing to reform from. What about my wild and reckless youth?

Suddenly it's not playful anymore; Sybil pushes Dorian away.

SYBIL *(Hurt)* Oh well, when you put it like that. *(Beat)* I suppose you've given up so much for me.

DORIAN Come on, Sybil, you know what I mean.

SYBIL Unfortunately I do. I'm holding you back.

DORIAN Holding me back?

SYBIL I've seen the pretty young groupies. I've read your fan mail. It's much more *(Beat)* explicit than anything I've ever got. I suppose I should be *grateful* you've been able to resist.

DORIAN I'm only interested in us doing something together.

SYBIL Do I need 'The Vanity of Vane: Volume 2'?

Dorian walks up behind her and touches her gently on the arm.

DORIAN I'm not talking about you going all the way back down that road. But let's have a few deliciously debauched adventures together.

SYBIL 'Deliciously debauched' that sounds like the sort of thing Harry would say.

Sybil turns to face Dorian.

DORIAN Oh, Sybil. *(Stroking her hair and looking into her eyes)* I know you want to. I can see it in your eyes. I can see it in the way your lips are twitching at the corner.

SYBIL Really?

Sybil runs her fingers down Dorian's chest.

SYBIL I suppose the idea of taking someone into our bed and seeing you with them *could* be quite a turn on.

DORIAN Another woman?

SYBIL Or man. Yes, I like the idea of a man.

DORIAN I wasn't expecting that.

SYBIL The road getting too scary already?

DORIAN Try me.

The cast clear the dressing table props and put them back in the wooden box.

ACT 3 – SCENE 2
THE BLUE TURTLE CLUB IN SOHO

There is a large 'Blue Turtle Club' noticeboard on the easel. This shows that this is a large place with lots going on and many rooms – cabaret, gaming tables, cocktail lounge and more. It also shows that this is late January 1966.

The lights are dim and moody. There is a smoky haze in the air.

A small club table, surrounded by 4 chairs, is set with a blue table lamp, a 'Blue Turtle Cocktail Bar' menu, matching coasters and a blue ashtray.

BASIL (In his 3-button suit and turtleneck) and HARRY (Wearing his sharp, shark skin suit) stand together towards the front of the stage. They each hold a cocktail. Basil has a dry martini, with a twist of lemon. Harry a Rusty Nail, with a cherry.

All around there is the jolly chatter of a popular club.

1960s psychedelic pop plays on the sound system.

BASIL *(Glancing around disapprovingly)* I really can't fathom why you insist on coming here, Harry. You know I've always loathed the place. And this martini cost nine shillings, nine shillings! *(Fishing the bit of lemon peel from his drink)* And I did ask for an olive.

HARRY High prices help keep the riff raff out and they do by far the best Rusty Nail this side of Berkeley Square. Anyway, Dorian suggested that we meet here, it's his favourite.

BASIL Dorian's favourite – nonsense! The only reason it hasn't been shut down is that it's run by gangsters with the police in their pocket. It's infested with drug dealers. There are rooms upstairs that are let by the hour. *(He glances round and spots something off to the left)* Look, those young women are blatantly snorting cocaine over there. I can't for the life of me imagine Dorian liking it here.

HARRY Oh, Basil, you're so naive. Perhaps he's taken to the place *because* of all of the above. That's certainly why they've the amusing cheek to charge nine shillings for a glass of gin with a drop of vermouth in it. *(Points at Basil's drink)* Anyway, you can quiz him yourself as to why he likes it…

DORIAN (Wearing a striped boating blouson & blue turtleneck) followed by ALAN (Wearing his tweed jacket & knitted bow tie) enter across the stage.

HARRY *(Gestures with his drink)* Here he comes now and he seems to have brought that adorable Alan Campbell with him.

Dorian and Alan reach Basil and Harry.

DORIAN *(Greeting them warmly)* Basil, Harry.

HARRY Dorian and with Alan. What a lovely surprise. Come and sit down.

ALAN *(Nodding and smiling at Harry, then Basil)* Thank you.

They all sit around the table. Harry and Basil sit next to each other in the middle. Dorian on the seat to stage right. Alan on the seat to stage left.

DORIAN I suddenly got the urge to see Alan, so I phoned and asked him to come along.

ALAN It was great to get your call, Dorian. I've been looking forward to seeing you again. *(Glancing round)* This is an *(beat)* interesting place.

DORIAN Yes, it is. It's my new favourite club.

HARRY *(Grinning at Basil)* What was that, Dorian?

DORIAN It's my new favourite club.

HARRY Yes, I thought that's what you said.

Basil forces a grin back at Harry.

DORIAN *(To Alan)* You were brilliant on 'Life Lab' last night. *(To Harry and Basil)* Did you see it?

BASIL I don't own a television set.

HARRY I saw it. It was riveting. Who'd have thought the ins and outs of chemistry could be so televisual? You take such an engrossing approach, Alan.

ALAN It's nothing, really.

BASIL Yes, I expect so. *(Turning to Dorian)* How's the formation of the band going?

DORIAN Slight change of plan there. I went to see The Animals at The Marquee a few weeks back and became very interested in one of the support bands, The Squad. So I intend joining them.

BASIL And how do the members of The Squad feel about this?

DORIAN They're very interested, actually, Basil. *(Beat)* Well, most of them are.

HARRY But there's a problem…?

DORIAN I want them to be billed as 'Dorian Gray and The Squad'. None of them seem especially keen on that bit. *(Beat)* The drummer's really digging his heels in.

ALAN Is the billing very important?

HARRY Of course it is. Find another band.

DORIAN No. I want this lot. The bass guitarist is of particular interest – a unique talent. I'll let them win me over, then it'll be a matter of getting rid of the drummer from within. We'll be 'Dorian Gray and The

Squad' by the time of our first gig.

HARRY That's the spirit.

BASIL What's happening to you, Dorian?

DORIAN Why do you always have be so bloody judgmental?

Dorian puts a cigarette in his mouth and lights it, maintaining defiant eye contact with Basil. He blows smoke from the corner of his mouth.

Basil looks both hurt and annoyed, but stubbornly holds Dorian's gaze.

Alan glances uncomfortably between Dorian and Basil, then quickly gets to his feet.

ALAN *(Clears his throat)* Can I get everyone a drink?

BASIL Thank you. A dry martini. Very dry, no lemon peel, just an olive.

ALAN *(Almost to himself, irritated)* Very dry, olive.

DORIAN I fancy a Champagne cocktail. Can you make certain they use five-star Hennessy and plenty of bitters?

ALAN *(Smiling warmly – pleased)* Anything you like, Dorian.

HARRY Nice idea. I'll have one too.

ALAN *(Beat)* Coming right up.

Alan picks up the tray and exits stage left, he glances back at Dorian as he goes.

Harry watches Alan until he is out of sight, then…

HARRY I think the lovely Alan has quite a crush on you, Dorian.

BASIL Don't be absurd, Harry.

DORIAN Do you think so?

HARRY Don't pretend you haven't noticed. You enjoy it. The question is, are you going to do anything about it?

DORIAN He's at odds with himself. I think he's far from comfortable with that part of his nature. Added to that, I don't think he's in the least bit confident as to what my reaction would be.

BASIL And what would your reaction be?

DORIAN Don't know. Perhaps if Sybil were here, we'd indulge together.

HARRY How intriguing. But Sybil isn't here. So let's just focus on you, shall we?

DORIAN *(Stubbing his cigarette out, smiling)* OK, Harry. I admit it – I do find him attractive.

HARRY But at this stage, he lacks assurance of this. Why don't you take him to one of the upstairs rooms and instil some confidence in him?

BASIL Harry, you can't know what you're saying. Dorian, don't listen to him.

HARRY Ask for room seven, it's more of a suite and available all night.

DORIAN As fun as that sounds, it's out of the question. It would be well outside the parameters of the arrangement I have with Sybil.

HARRY So, you and Sybil have an arrangement, do you? This gets more fascinating by the second.

BASIL For God's sake. You'll both regret this conversation, I'm sure of that.

HARRY Two attractive young men, and possibly the gorgeous Sybil too – my only regret is that I won't be able to watch. *(Beat)* Flirt with him, Dorian. I want to see how he reacts. Let's find out how far this could go.

BASIL Oh come on. If Alan's as smitten as you suggest, is it fair to toy with him like that? *(Turning to*

Dorian) Anyway, if this got out of hand, the pair of you could end up being arrested and then where…

HARRY *(Interrupting)* Hardly likely. This is the Blue Turtle. All the suffocating laws of the land come to a screeching halt just shy of the cloakroom.

BASIL Yeah, clearly.

Alan returns carrying the small tray with three Champagne cocktails and a dry martini, with a lemon twist and no olive. He has an innocent smile, oblivious to the conversation. He hands out the drinks and places the tray to one side.

ALAN I was tempted too. *(Picks up a Champagne cocktail)* The bitters and the sugar should have an exciting reaction. Nice choice, Dorian.

Basil plucks the lemon peel from his glass, looks at it sourly, then tosses it into the ashtray.

DORIAN *(Making firm eye contact with Alan)* Thank you. *(He takes a sip)* Mmm, just how I like it.

HARRY Yes, very moreish. *(Raising his glass)* Cheers. Now, I for one intend taking full advantage of the perks of this place. I'm following the lead of the sensible young ladies over there.

Harry goes into his pocket and takes out a small bottle with a silver top and a tiny spoon.

HARRY *(As he unscrews the bottle top)* I'm having a little cocaine chaser with my Champagne cocktail.

Harry then snorts a small spoonful of cocaine up each nostril.

BASIL Oh, Harry!

HARRY Dorian, care to join me?

DORIAN *(Taking the bottle and spoon)* Sounds perfect.

Dorian snorts some cocaine.

HARRY And what about you, Alan?

Basil puts down his glass and folds his arms with a deeply irritated sigh.

ALAN *(Looking at Dorian)* I don't think I *(beat)* should. *(Alan looks around nervously)*

DORIAN Go on, try a little, for me.

Alan, tempted now, again looks around nervously.

Dorian hands over the bottle and spoon, flirtatiously touching Alan's hand as he does so.

Alan smiles warmly at Dorian as he snorts a spoonful of cocaine.

ACT 3 – SCENE 3
THE BEDROOM IN SYBIL'S HOUSE

The lights are low. The same 1960s psychedelic rock from the previous scene can be heard playing in the background.

The dressing table is set with a hand mirror, a hairbrush, makeup box, perfume atomiser, a jar of cold cream and a bottle of pills. There is also a bottle of Dimple Haig whisky, 3 glasses with whisky in them, a packet of cocaine, a mirror and straw. Near this is an envelope containing a solicitor's letter.

DORIAN (dressed as the previous scene but without his shoes and socks) and ALAN (also dressed as the previous scene but without his bow tie, shoes and socks) stand centre stage in an embrace. They kiss and pull off each other's jackets.

Sybil (wearing a short dressing gown over her underwear) sits at the dressing table watching Dorian and Alan. She then snorts a line of cocaine from a small mirror and takes a swig of whisky.

Sybil gets up and walks over to Alan. He turns away from Dorian to face her. She takes off his glasses as he unbuttons his shirt. Sybil then embraces Alan and kisses him.

Dorian pulls off his turtleneck and watches Sybil and Alan. He goes to the dressing table, sits, snorts some cocaine and takes a swig of whisky. He then removes his trousers before moving back over to Sybil.

Sybil turns to face Dorian, he pushes her dressing gown off her shoulders so that it falls to the floor.

They then embrace and kiss.

Alan watches this, now sitting on the bed taking off his trousers.

Sybil and Dorian sit on the bed next to Alan, with Dorian in the middle. Sybil and Alan turn to Dorian kiss and embrace him together. The three fall back on the bed and huddle together.

The lights dim to blackout. After a moment, the psychedelic rock music fades and…

The lights go back up. The room is brighter now – it is the morning.

Sybil, Dorian and Alan are still in bed. They are all asleep. Then…

Alan opens his eyes. He sits up and looks at Dorian and Sybil. He seems sleepy and dazed but manages to reach out for his watch to check the time. He squints at the watch then reaches for his glasses…

ALAN *(Panicking)* Oh God…oh no…Jesus Christ!

Alan jumps from the bed and starts to get dressed.

Dorian sits up.

DORIAN You off?

ALAN *(Hurriedly)* I'm so sorry, but I've got to go.

DORIAN *(Rubbing his eyes)* Go?

ALAN I'm late for a recording. I should've been at Television Centre… *(looks at the watch again)* two minutes ago. I've got to get to White City and it'll take half an hour in a cab. Sorry.

DORIAN Don't be sorry, I understand. You go, we'll speak soon.

Alan now has his trousers and an unbuttoned shirt on. He dashes back to the bed and gives Dorian a loving, slow kiss.

ALAN Thanks, Dorian. I'll phone tonight.

Alan hurries out of the room, attempting to button his shirt properly as he goes. He exits stage left.

Sybil wakes up, rubs her eyes and yawns.

SYBIL *(Massaging her temples)* Oh God, some sadistic bastard seems to have forced a ball of barbed wire right inside of my skull. It's lacerating my brain every time I move my head.

DORIAN Can I get you anything?

SYBIL Yes, a hundred paracetamol and a neck brace. *(Looking around)* Where's Alan?

DORIAN He just left. He's late for the sacred BBC.

SYBIL Give me a kiss. *(They kiss)* You were very forceful with him last night. Much more so than you ever are with me.

DORIAN Too forceful?

SYBIL He seemed to like it.

DORIAN He did, didn't he. Would you like me to be more like that with you?

SYBIL *(Coldly not looking at Dorian)* No, I love the way we are together. It's perfect.

Sybil pulls on her dressing gown and gets out of bed.

SYBIL *(As she does so)* Christ, I feel as if I belong on a slab.

She goes over to the dressing table and sits. She takes a swig from a glass, draining it – a Scotch left from last night. She then grabs the bottle and starts to pour another.

DORIAN *(Watching her)* Isn't it a bit early for that?

SYBIL Actually, it's late, too late.

DORIAN *(Getting out of bed and putting on his*

dressing gown) What do you mean?

SYBIL *(Holding up a sheet of paper)* I got this letter from my solicitor yesterday. The independent medical report is in and they still suspect *(Reading from the letter)* "substance abuse and alcohol dependency". The custody hearing has been indefinitely suspended. They suggest we try again in twelve months.

Sybil hands the letter to Dorian over her shoulder. She gazes at herself in the mirror. Her expression is blank.

With Sybil's back turned, Dorian reads the letter and develops a small smile; he's secretly pleased with the news. He then then quickly controls his face and adopts a more serious expression.

DORIAN Are you going to challenge it?

SYBIL I might have done, if it wasn't all true. *(Beat)* Anyway, I'd better liven myself up. I've got to be at rehearsals in an hour.

Sybil takes the small mirror with the cocaine and snorts a line through a straw.

DORIAN *(Studying Sybil as he puts the letter back on the dressing table)* Are you all right?

SYBIL I've got to be, haven't I?

Sybil starts to put on her makeup.

DORIAN Perhaps it's all for the best. What time have we got for a child right now? The play opens in less than a week, and it's bound to have a long run. The band's at a crucial stage and there's talk of a tour…

Dorian stands behind Sybil and places a hands on her shoulders, softly massaging them.

DORIAN …Next year sounds about right to me – things will be different then. *(Beat)* Trust me.

ACT 3 – SCENE 4
THE LIVING ROOM IN SYBIL'S HOUSE

The easel and painting are to the front of stage right, facing away from the audience.

There are a few open bottles of Champagne positioned about the stage, together with some glasses. One bottle is placed on a small table to stage left.

HARRY (Wearing his dinner jacket and diamond cut bow tie) and BASIL (Wearing his 3-button suit, white turtleneck and Breton cap) stand together at centre stage chatting. They each have a glass of Champagne.

MAVIS (Wearing high 1960s fashion) stands off to stage right and ALAN (wearing his tweed jacket and bow tie) stands off to stage left. They too hold glasses of Champagne.

Jazz plays softly. The lights are low. There is a smoky haze in the air. There is the sound of the chatter of other guests, but this time it is sparse and subdued.

HARRY *(Glancing round)* Not a very good turnout for an after press night party at the star's own home.

BASIL Word's got round. The previews.

HARRY So, what did you think of Sybil and 'The Female Factory'?

BASIL I felt sorry for her.

HARRY Don't be such a bitch, Basil.

BASIL I didn't mean it like that. My heart went out to her tonight. I desperately wanted it to be better, for her sake.

HARRY I've always had the impression you had no time for Sybil. More so since Dorian's arrival.

BASIL I'm allowed to change my mind and I have done with Sybil. It's obvious she genuinely cares for Dorian – she loves him. She also genuinely cares for her art. That's why this will be hurting her profoundly. I understand how all of that feels.

ALAN (*Moving closer to Basil and Harry.*) When will we know what the critics have said?

HARRY (*Helping himself to more Champagne*) Soon.

MAVIS (*Glancing at her watch*) The early editions will have already gone to press by now.

ALAN I think I should get my coat and go. I can't see Dorian or Sybil anywhere.

MAVIS They'll have to show their faces at some stage, surely.

HARRY (*Topping up Alan's glass*) Yes, they're bound to turn up sooner or later. They do live here after all.

BASIL Perhaps it would be best if we grabbed this chance to just slip away before…

HARRY (*With an amused smile*) Too late.

The music stops abruptly.

Harry gestures with his glass towards...

SYBIL enters wearing an ivory silk dress and matching coat. She is carrying a thick pile of newspapers.

SYBIL (*As she marches in*) Guess what, gang? The reviews are in! This should be entertaining.

She plonks the newspapers onto the small table, next to the Champagne.

DORIAN wearing a black dinner jacket and an undone bow tie enters. He stands back and watches Sybil in silence, arms folded.

48

SYBIL Let's see what kind and encouraging comments the gentlemen of the press have to contribute, shall we? *(Picking up a newspaper and opening it)* Ah yes, this one. "Sybil Vane gives the best performance of Martha from 'Who's Afraid of Virginia Woolf' this reviewer has ever seen. Unfortunately, she's appearing in a new play called 'The Female Factory', perhaps somebody should tell her." *(She slams down the newspaper)* Charming! *(She picks up another newspaper)* And then there was this, "Sybil Vane: In the kitchen sink and all washed up." *(She bitterly sniggers to herself)* You've got to hand it to him, that one is rather witty. Anyway, I shan't go on, you get the idea, I'm certain.

Sybil slams down the second newspaper.

Mavis dashes over, seemingly concerned.

MAVIS There, there, Sybil. *(She puts an arm round Sybil's shoulders)* You can't win them all. Let me get you a nice drink.

SYBIL *(Pushing Mavis's arm away)* Who the bloody hell let you in?

MAVIS Am I not welcome?

SYBIL You'd only be welcome in here if the house was on fire.

MAVIS What?

SYBIL Get out, Mavis. And by the way, I hope you have a massive embolism.

MAVIS *(Grinning and nodding)* I can see now why you've been deemed an unfit mother.

SYBIL *(She sniggers bitterly to herself again for a moment, then…)* Fuck off. *(To the whole room)* In fact, all of you can get out!

The guests all start glancing at each other confused.

SYBIL *(Much more aggressively)* I said, get out!

Dorian continues to watch in silence, arms folded.

The guests glance at each other, put down their drinks then start to exit stage left. They each say a quiet 'good night' or just nod to Dorian as they pass.

Basil seems about to say something to Sybil, but then thinks better of it and simply leaves with everyone else.

Dorian smiles and nods to each of them as they go.

Harry, however, hasn't moved. He takes another sip of Champagne.

Sybil strides over and takes Harry's glass…

SYBIL That means you too, Harry.

HARRY I'll speak to you tomorrow, Dorian. Goodnight, Sybil.

Harry exits stage left.

Sybil downs the remains of Harry's drink herself.

DORIAN *(Watching Sybil, blankly)* Well, I must say that was a smart way to extract even more venom from everyone. Not to mention lose the few friends we've got left.

SYBIL Friends? They can go to hell.

DORIAN No, Sybil. We're the ones going to hell.

SYBIL We! We! Since when did any of this affect you? I'm the one with the freshly clipped ticket to oblivion. Now I get word that both the film roles I was after are going to Julie bloody Christie. Both!

DORIAN *(Pouring a drink)* She is very good.

SYBIL Good! Yes, and young and fuckable. Get Harry to introduce you. Not what I wanted to hear, Dorian. And take a look at me, I've aged 10 years since I accepted this part. 10 years in 10 months.

DORIAN I feel the same.

SYBIL Rubbish. You look exactly like you do in that painting. *(She points at the canvass)* No, if anything, you look even younger!

DORIAN Younger than I do in the painting?

SYBIL Yes, you're actually even more fresh-faced, even more youthful.

DORIAN Nonsense, we're exactly alike.

SYBIL And Basil has made your eyes look rather cruel and distant. It had never struck me before, but I noticed it the other day.

DORIAN Well, that certainly isn't true. The eyes were the last thing he completed. I've looked into them a thousand times. Cruel and distant – no.

Sybil strides over to a bottle of Champagne and pours herself a glass.

SYBIL *(Flicking her head in the direction of the painting)* Take a look for yourself, if you don't believe me.

Dorian approaches the painting. He leans in and narrows his eyes.

DORIAN Good God, you're right. Why've I never noticed this before?

SYBIL Told you.

DORIAN And my face doesn't seem to glow the way it used to. *(Glancing around)* Is the sunlight getting at it or something?

SYBIL I wouldn't have thought so. It was oh so carefully positioned to avoid that sort of thing.

DORIAN *(Annoyed and confused)* Well, something's happened to it.

SYBIL I think now that the novelty's worn off, we're simply starting to notice that there are little bits of cynicism in Basil's representation of your good looks;

a sort of satire hidden there. I wouldn't put it past him.

DORIAN *(Defensive)* I don't believe that. There isn't and never has been anything cynical in the way Basil sees me. He adores and admires me and my appearance. It's all very pure and he put that into the picture.

SYBIL Pure! Don't make me laugh. There's nothing *pure* in Basil's thoughts about you. Anyway, how'd this conversation become all about you and that fucking painting? I wish I'd never set eyes on the thing. I wish nobody'd ever set eyes on it.

DORIAN Now we're getting to the truth. You're jealous.

SYBIL Jealous – of you or the painting? *(Putting her hands on her hips)* I am jealous of the way you evidently feel about it. I've seen you mooning over the thing. I think it's a particularly sick kind of narcissism.

DORIAN Do you?

SYBIL Yes. I think looking at it arouses you.

DORIAN It's no secret that I love the painting. For me it was the genesis of everything good. It changed my life overnight.

SYBIL It changed you alright.

DORIAN It opened my eyes.

SYBIL Opened them to what exactly?

DORIAN Do you really want to know?

SYBIL *(Cautiously)* Yes.

DORIAN Alright. *(Beat)* You once said you were holding me back. Well, it's worse than that, you're dragging me down.

SYBIL How dare you!

DORIAN And now you've disappointed me terribly.

Dorian picks up a bottle of Champagne and pours himself another glass.

DORIAN *(With his back to Sybil)* In fact, I've recently realised I no longer love you.

SYBIL What?

Dorian turns and moves in very close to Sybil.

DORIAN There's no respect left, you see. You failed to deliver on the mundane – a family life with little Hetty is out of the question – we should stop deluding ourselves. And you failed to deliver on the extraordinary – 'The Female Factory' is a disaster and that's down to *(Prodding Sybil with his finger as he speaks)* you and your sloppy, screechy performance. I can't sit in that theatre night after night and feel nothing but embarrassment – it would be torture.

Sybil slaps Dorian's face.

SYBIL *(Devastated but trying to hide it)* Well, you can get lost too. Just like the rest of those vacuous arseholes.

DORIAN That's exactly what I intend to do. Anyway, people like us don't stay together for life. We were bound to separate eventually. We've had our fun. It's better we call it a day now before the contempt and spitefulness really take root.

SYBIL *(Almost to herself)* So it's over, just like that?

DORIAN Quite over.

SYBIL I see. *(Beat)* Don't you worry, I'll make it easy for you.

DORIAN Of course, you've had experience with divorce.

SYBIL *(Through a silent laugh)* You bastard!

DORIAN I'm leaving you now, Sybil. *(Walking away from Sybil and heading for his exit stage left)* I won't be back.

SYBIL Really?

DORIAN Really.

Dorian exits, he does not look back.

SYBIL *(Calling after him)* Mind how you go! *(Softly, sorrowful)* Take care, Dorian.

1960's psychedelic rock begins to play.

Sybil swigs back her drink then takes off her coat and tosses it aside.

She clumsily pours herself another drink, splashing some onto the table.

She goes over to the painting, looking at it with contempt, then raises her glass to it in a mock toast.

She swigs back most of her drink and is soon refilling the glass.

Sybil seems a bit drunk now – she sways to the music, the drink in one hand, the other hand caressing her throat. Her eyes are closed.

She drains her glass again with a few quick gulps, then slumps into a chair: As she does so, the empty glass drops from her hand.

ACT 3 – SCENE 5
A PRIVATE ROOM
(NUMBER SEVEN)
THE BLUE TURTLE CLUB

DORIAN is asleep on a bed, dressed only in his underwear.

Dorian's dinner suit, shirt and shoes are strewn over the floor. There is an almost finished bottle of vodka, 3 glasses and a mirror with some traces of cocaine. There is also a small piece of paper on the floor near the bed.

HARRY (Wearing his sharkskin suit, op-art tie and Crombie overcoat) is standing over the bed looking down at Dorian. He reaches down and takes Dorian gently by the arm.

Dorian wakes up suddenly.

DORIAN *(Startled)* Jesus Christ, Harry!

HARRY Good morning, Dorian.

DORIAN *(Sitting up, thrown)* How the bloody hell did you get in here?

HARRY Oh, you'll find that the staff at the Blue Turtle will do anything for me.

DORIAN *(Rubbing his eyes)* What, including letting you into *supposedly* private rooms?

HARRY Yes, including that.

DORIAN For fuck's sake, Harry, what do you want?

HARRY What do I want? Half of London is looking for you.

DORIAN And the other half doesn't give a fuck.

Dorian flops back on the bed.

Harry sits down on the bed next to Dorian.

HARRY Dorian, I'm so very sorry about Sybil. It's all just terrible.

DORIAN You've heard?

HARRY Yes, it's already quite public knowledge, I'm afraid.

DORIAN Of course it is. Anyway, it's nothing to get het up about, it's all going to be fine… *(He lights a cigarette)*

HARRY Fine? How could it possibly be fine?

DORIAN I know I can put this right.

HARRY *(Confused)* Put this right?

DORIAN *(Sitting back up)* I'll speak to her as soon as I can; beg her forgiveness and then we'll live happily ever after. That's what I really want. It's all very clear to me now.

HARRY What are you talking about?

DORIAN This might all seem so dramatic at the moment, but by tonight, she and I will be back to normal. You… and everyone else will see. That's all…

HARRY *(Cutting in. Grabs Dorian's upper arms and forces strong eye-contact)* Dorian, Dorian, listen to me, listen to me. *(Deep breath)* Sybil is *(Beat)* dead.

DORIAN What?

HARRY Sybil is dead.

DORIAN *(Pulling away from Harry's grip)* Don't make sick jokes like that, Harry.

HARRY *(A little breathless)* I wish it were a joke. I'm so very sorry.

DORIAN *(Softly, slowly, dazed)* I can't believe it.

HARRY The authorities have been frantically trying to contact you since the body was found. I assumed they must have done by now, and that you'd sought refuge here. *(Beat)* The press are having a feeding frenzy out there.

DORIAN *(Still in a daze)* After she chucked you lot out, we argued, badly. *(Beat)* I said things that were unspeakably cruel, *(Beat)* and enjoyed it, (beat) I did. *(Beat)* Then I left. *(Beat)* I've been here all night.

HARRY I see.

DORIAN What… what happened?

HARRY It's not clear, yet. Possibly an accident, possibly *(beat)* suicide. They have established that it was some kind of barbiturate poisoning.

Dorian seems to fall into deep thought for a moment, nodding, processing. He gets up and walks to the front of the stage. He stubs out his cigarette then stares ahead, unblinking. He seems almost serene.

DORIAN *(Calmly)* I'm frightened.

HARRY *(Walking up behind Dorian)* There's no need to be frightened.

DORIAN Oh, but there is. I'm frightened of myself. You see, I don't really feel very much about this. Don't you think I should worry about that fact?

HARRY You're in shock.

DORIAN *(Calm)* No, it's not that. I keep thinking 'how should I feel?', but without actually feeling anything. *(Beat)* There should at least be some sort of remorse, I suppose, considering that I murdered her.

Harry gets to his feet and walks up behind Dorian.

HARRY Murdered her? No you didn't, don't say that. You must *never* say that.

DORIAN *(Still calm)* I did though. I may as well have forced the pills down her throat myself.

HARRY *(With urgency)* Dorian, it could certainly have been an accident. Nobody's going to find the idea of Sybil downing too many pills attempting to get smashed that incredible.

DORIAN Yes, and I'd be the one who drove her to it. Again, murder.

HARRY *(Taking Dorian by the upper arms and forcing him round so that they face each other)* Look, look! The police are bound to want to speak to you sometime today. For fuck's sake keep this indulgent bullshit about *murder* to yourself!

DORIAN *(Pulling away from Harry's grip)* Of course I will.

Dorian starts picking up his clothes.

HARRY It's also bloody useful there'll be ample proof that you've been here all night.

DORIAN *(Pulling on his trousers)* Proof?

HARRY The staff at the club… and I take it you weren't alone in that bed.

DORIAN *(Putting on his shirt)* Yes, I had company. They both left early this morning.

HARRY With the involvement of the law, I can only hope they're women and they'll be contactable.

DORIAN Sisters, their number's by the bed.

Harry picks up the small bit of paper from near the bed and looks at it.

HARRY All good. *(He slips the paper into his wallet)* There'll be a dreadful scandal, of course. But we can easily turn that sort of notoriety to our advantage.

DORIAN Advantage?

HARRY This is all very tragic, hideous, sad. But you're the one who has to live on and that life can't become tragic, hideous and sad – no. Something constructive can come out of this unholy mess, given a bit of time. We focus on that.

DORIAN *(Getting to his feet and buckling his belt)* How can anything good possibly come out of this?

HARRY It's the sort of thing that'll get locked in the public's imagination forever – the gorgeous rock star from the famous painting caught up in this appallingly ugly tragedy. Sex and death all tinged with tantalising ambiguity. There'll be the most salacious gossip, of course – it's such a potent story.

DORIAN *(Thoughtful, resigning)* A story.

HARRY Yes, a story that they'll want more of. More of Dorian Gray. Hungry for the next chapter.

DORIAN *(Now fully dressed. His voice concerned)* What have you got in mind, Harry?

HARRY Once everyone's horror and sorrow has worn off, this could end up the stuff that legends are made of – if handled properly. *(Beat)* You gotta use the death of Sybil Vane – let it infect your art… for a while. Write and record a song that's a thinly-veiled, melancholic account of this experience. It doesn't have to be that sincere, just as long as it's there and open to that interpretation. *(Beat)* It'll be a sensation, Dorian! A sensation!

Dorian walks back to the front of the stage, deep in thought.

Harry follows, until he stands just behind him.

DORIAN *(Looking blankly ahead)* Oh Harry, I understand what you're suggesting… I do. *(Beat)* And no; I won't go there… Not there.

Harry turns and walks away frustrated.

ACT 3 – SCENE 6
THE LIVING ROOM IN SYBIL'S HOUSE

The easel is at the front of stage right facing away from the audience, but now there is no picture on the easel.

There are a number of open bottles of Champagne about the stage, together with numerous Champagne glasses; the remnants of last night's party.

DORIAN (still in his dinner suit with an undone bow tie) enters from stage left. He takes off his jacket and tosses it onto a seat. He then pours himself a glass of Champagne. He looks across at the empty easel.

HARRY and BASIL enter.

DORIAN *(As they approach)* Harry, Basil – You came.

HARRY Of course we came.

BASIL You should be with your friends at a time like this.

DORIAN Thank you. Thank you both.

BASIL *(Looking at the easel then around, perplexed)* Where's the painting?

DORIAN I've had it moved to… *(Beat)* another part of the house.

BASIL What? Since last night? With all that's been going on here?

Dorian walks over to the easel, reaches out and touches it gently.

DORIAN *(As he does so)* Yes. With the way Sybil felt about the painting… *(Beat)* and what happened to her in this room; it's become just too upsetting, too intensely private to have on display in here. *(Turning back to face Basil)* I'm sure you understand.

BASIL *(Slightly confused)* Oh… Yes… I see. I thought that you might…

HARRY *(Cutting in)* Stop sulking about your bloody painting, Basil. You've got the real Dorian right here in front of you. Don't be so greedy.

Dorian glances back and forth between Harry and Basil. Then…

DORIAN Harry, I wanted to tell you about a decision I've made. *(Beat)* I'm going to be able to write that song you suggested after all. Actually, it's going to be a whole concept album.

HARRY A concept album. *(Subtly excited)* Oh, now that is some good news. I knew you had it in you.

BASIL I'm glad you've found something to occupy your mind. Something creative. Perhaps it will help.

DORIAN Yes. I'm expecting this to be quite a turning point for me.

Basil starts to take off his jacket.

DORIAN Don't take that off, Basil. We're going out. Deciding to embark on this new project has put me in the mood to celebrate and drink plenty of obscenely expensive Champagne. I've booked our favourite table at the Ad Lib. Let's paint this town scarlet.

BASIL You're suggesting we go out on the town? Tonight? Quaffing Champagne? You can't be serious.

DORIAN I'm being perfectly serious. I don't want this day to slip by without marking it properly.

BASIL Harry, talk to him, make him see sense.

HARRY No.

BASIL What?

HARRY I'm in complete agreement with Dorian. Today he's committed to make this album – it's the beginning of the most glorious future. We'll never have tonight again; we should do as he says and celebrate thoroughly.

DORIAN Thank you, Harry. You're a true friend.

BASIL What? I can only imagine that this must be the grief and the shock talking. But sorry, Dorian, I won't be part of it. And, Harry, you can do what you like. You usually do!

Basil exits briskly.

Dorian and Harry watch him go, as they do so…

DORIAN *(Annoyed, but softly)* Good riddance. He'd have only put a damper on the whole occasion.

HARRY Very true. But he was right about one thing…

Harry goes to a bottle of Champagne and pours them a glass each.

HARRY …we shouldn't go out. We can celebrate here tonight, away from the prying eyes of pious scrutiny. Conventional minds may not see the funny side of it.

Dorian chuckles silently to himself.

DORIAN What would I do without you, Harry?

HARRY You never have to be without me.

They join each other at centre stage and Harry hands Dorian a glass.

HARRY Let's drink to the future, your future. *(Raising his glass)* You're going to soar, Dorian – like an angel on the wing.

DORIAN Oh, I know, Harry… I know *(Clinking glasses).*

INTERVAL

ACT 4 – SCENE 1
LWT TELEVISION STUDIO
SOUTH BANK, LONDON
1977

The 'Mavis Meets…' theme music plays. It sounds very late 1970's disco influenced.

The Lights go up.

The easel is at the rear of stage right, now with a large sign showing the "Mavis Meets…" logo on it.

MAVIS (Wearing a strikingly patterned 1970s maxi dress) sits in her chat show chair. Her hair colour and style has changed. She looks a little older, but is covering it up well.

DORIAN (Wearing a black leather jacket, yellow t-shirt and flared black jeans) sits beside her. Now his hair is slicked back, but otherwise looks exactly the same.

After a few moments the music fades and…

MAVIS *(To the audience)* What can one say about my next guest? Some have likened him to a celestial being sent down from heaven. Others have described him as the devil himself, a corrupting influence on the youth of today. We knew what he looked like before we'd even heard him sing a note. After his smash hit concept album, the heartbreaking 'Fallen Star', he transformed himself into the crown prince of glam rock and again took the charts by storm. More recently, he's been making his mark across the Atlantic with yet another style of music. Now, 1977 sees him back in the UK with a brand new album. But what was hidden under all that glitter and makeup? Who is the man behind the image? We're about to find out as Mavis Meets Dorian Gray!

Mavis turns to Dorian.

MAVIS Welcome to 'Mavis Meets', Dorian.

DORIAN *(With a warm smile)* It's good to be here.

MAVIS We've been trying to get you on the show for some time.

DORIAN Have you?

MAVIS Yes. *(Beat)* Now, I think it would be fair to say that controversy follows you around.

DORIAN *(Frowning)* You might think it's 'fair'.

MAVIS Well, you surely must agree that you're never far from a sensational headline. But I'm attempting to find out if there's any truth behind the stories.

DORIAN Is that what you're doing?

MAVIS It is *(Beat)* but you're not being very forthcoming.

DORIAN Try asking some questions. So far it's been a series of statements.

MAVIS So you do understand that this is supposed to be an interview.

DORIAN Interview? It's an irrelevant farce, that's what this is.

MAVIS Just checking that you understand what's going on here. That you haven't taken anything that has… well, let's just say, transported you elsewhere.

DORIAN If only.

MAVIS Let's move on to your new album, 'The White Night'.

DORIAN Let's.

MAVIS It's a challenging listen, to say the least. With Glam Rock a thing of the past, perhaps you should face up to the fact that you're a thing of the past too.

DORIAN *(Laughs for a moment then...)* I've had it with this preposterous waste of time. Why don't you go fuck yourself?

Dorian storms off and exits stage left.

MAVIS Well! *(Getting to her feet and waving her arms)* Stop recording! Stop recording!

Mavis moves to centre stage.

After a moment, Dorian strolls back on smiling.

DORIAN How was that?

MAVIS Totally convincing. *(They embrace)* It'll go out on Saturday night's show with a bleep over the 'fuck' and it'll be in all the papers come Sunday morning. I've already written up my article. It's very effective – I tell of my shock and distress.

DORIAN Thank you, Mavis, you're a total darling.

HARRY (Wearing a brown leather jacket, a wide 1970s brown & orange tie and gold-framed sunglasses) enters from stage left.

HARRY *(Clapping his hands)* Perfect, just perfect!

DORIAN I thought you'd like it.

HARRY And, Mavis. What a performance.

MAVIS You know me, anything to help.

HARRY Yes. I've always admired your altruistic nature. Not a thought about reviving your dwindling ratings in any of this.

MAVIS *(Chuckles, then…)* Oh, Harry, I pity your relentless cynicism, I really do. *(Through a fake fixed smile)* Anyway, must dash. Catch you both later.

Mavis exits stage left.

HARRY *(Watches her go then, turns back to Dorian)* Next I think we should stir up the indignation of Mary Whitehouse.

DORIAN Agreed. I'm already working on getting the single banned by Radio One.

HARRY Are you now? Very nice. Let's conspire some more over a few drinks.

DORIAN I fancy a night at 'The Blue Turtle'.

HARRY It's no longer 'The Blue Turtle', I'm afraid. They're calling it 'Rags' these days.

They head for the exit stage left. As they go…

DORIAN Any good?

HARRY It's not what it was, but it has its charms.

ACT 4 – SCENE 2
DORIAN'S HOUSE (FORMERLY SYBIL'S HOUSE)

The lights at the front of the stage go up, the rear of the stage is left in darkness.

BASIL (Wearing a donkey jacket and heavy-knit pullover) enters from stage left. He looks at his watch and glances around.

After a moment, Basil moves to stage right and takes a swig from a hip flask. He looks at his watch again and takes another swig.

Dorian (Wearing his black leather jacket and yellow t-shirt – as previous scene) enters stage left.

DORIAN *(As he approaches)* Basil, what are you doing here?

BASIL *(Standing)* I called round, you weren't in.

DORIAN I've been out with Harry. *(Glancing at his watch)* It's quite late… is there anything wrong?

BASIL No. There's nothing wrong.

Dorian studies Basil's face for a moment then…

DORIAN Anyway, come inside.

Basil follows Dorian as he heads upstage and…

The lights above the rest of the stage go up revealing a small table set with a cocktail pitcher filled with ice, strainer and stirrer, olives on cocktail sticks, 2 cocktail glasses and a collection of bottles.

Music begins to play softly: Rather 1970s sounding slow and cool jazz funk.

Dorian walks over to the table.

DORIAN This is a nice surprise. It's been too long.

BASIL It's not been for the want of trying on my part.

DORIAN Well, we're together now.

DORIAN *(Picking up a bottle of gin)* What can I get you? A dry martini – no lemon peel, just an olive? That's right, yes?

BASIL *(Taking off his donkey jacket)* I stopped drinking them a while ago now. *(Beat)* But yes, tonight I think I will have a dry martini; for old times' sake.

Dorian is making the drinks – pouring the gin and vermouth into the cocktail pitcher.

DORIAN *(As he does so)* What have you been up to?

BASIL No painting to speak of. Nothing seems to inspire me anymore.

DORIAN *(Stirring the pitcher)* That's a shame.

BASIL I intend taking myself away travelling. I'm hoping that'll help.

DORIAN *(Straining the drinks into two cocktail glasses)* It may well do. I know that living in different parts of the world has affected my music enormously and for the better… mostly. Any idea where you'd like to end up?

Dorian plonks an olive on a stick into each glass and then hands Basil one of the drinks.

BASIL Not yet, perhaps I'll know when I get there.

They clink glasses.

BASIL Cheers.

DORIAN Cheers.

BASIL In the meantime, there's to be a retrospective of my work at the Hayward.

DORIAN Well, that is exciting.

BASIL Yeah, I've been going over all my available paintings with the curator and his team for weeks and everyone agrees that the centrepiece should be The Picture of Dorian Gray.

DORIAN And does *'everyone'* include you?

BASIL Yes.

DORIAN You said you'd never display it publicly.

BASIL That was a long time ago. It's the best thing I've ever done and I'm coming to the conclusion, the best thing I'll ever do.

DORIAN It's certainly remarkable. But sorry, I'm going to have to say 'no'.

BASIL Excuse me?

DORIAN It's quite out of the question, I'm afraid.

The jazz funk music fades.

BASIL I know there are emotional factors at play concerning the picture. I mean, I do remember that you stopped displaying it here in the living room soon after Sybil's… accident. But I would…

DORIAN *(Interrupting)* Accident! She committed suicide, Basil.

BASIL That was never really established. I would have thought that you'd have preferred to think of it as an accident. I know I do and there's every reason to believe it was just that…

DORIAN *(Interrupting)* She killed herself in total desperation, because she mistakenly thought she'd lost me forever.

BASIL That's horrible.

DORIAN It was the despair of Juliet. Where she became one of the great tragedies of our age. You nor anyone else will take that away by branding it as some common mishap.

BASIL I didn't mean any disrespect; I'm sorry. *(Beat)* Perhaps we should talk a bit more about you lending me back the painting. You see I…

DORIAN *(Interrupting)* Basil, I've said 'no'! If you persist in this, I swear I'll cut you out of my life permanently. You'll never see me again. I will do it. *(Beat)* I've done it to others and I'll do it to you.

BASIL God, you know how to threaten me effectively, don't you?

DORIAN You'd get over it.

BASIL Would I? *(Takes a sip of the drink)* You once said that my paintings reveal as much of me as they do of the subjects I paint. That's true, I suppose, and none more so than The Picture of Dorian Gray. You see, to me, it's an explicit testament to the fact that I madly desire you. All of you, mind and body – always have. Once we became friends, I tried desperately to keep those feelings all to myself – a heavy secret. But as I painted, they were exposed in every brush stroke, recorded in every mark of pigment. When I looked at the finished painting, I genuinely believed it would betray me; make all my longings utterly evident to anyone who looked at it. Feelings like that were dangerous then – illegal. So I decided that the picture should be… I don't know… something like a private correspondence between us. I took such joy in making it my gift to you. Little did I know then that… oh, well… never mind…

Dorian eats the olive from his drink and drops the stick back into his glass.

BASIL …Now I take fulfilment from the times when we're together; knowing it was you and I who created the picture. I cherish every second we share.

DORIAN I see. Thank you for finally confiding in me. It makes many things very clear.

BASIL It wasn't so much a confidence as a confession.

DORIAN But what have you really confessed? That you've lusted after me for years. I've always suspected it and now I know for certain. I think you've wanted all the young men in your pictures and that has influenced the way you've painted them. With me, it was more so, it's as simple as that.

Dorian takes the olive from Basil's glass and eats it.

Basil doesn't even notice this.

BASIL Don't trivialise it, Dorian.

DORIAN *(Chewing)* But it is trivial. This exaggerated importance exists only in your mind.

BASIL It's the way I am.

Dorian drops the olive stick back into Basil's drink – plonk!

DORIAN I know. I don't think I've ever met anyone so brave in their art, yet so cowardly in their personal life. To me, you seem not to have actually lived at all. You stubbornly resist experience at every turn.

BASIL You're being very harsh with me, Dorian. *(Beat)* I didn't intend to tell you any of this tonight. I didn't intend to ever tell you. I only came here to ask about displaying the painting. My painting.

DORIAN *(With controlled anger)* It's my painting!

Dorian turns his back on Basil and takes a few steps away. He puts down his glass, then turns back.

DORIAN OK, Basil, I've decided to give you what you want. Come upstairs with me to my bedroom and you can have it.

BASIL Your bedroom? *(Beat)* Is that where the painting is now?

Dorian chuckles softly for a moment, then...

DORIAN The painting. *(Beat)* Yes, that's where it is.

Dorian makes for stage left.

DORIAN Come.

Basil swigs back the remains of his drink, puts down the glass and follows Dorian.

They both exit.

ACT 4 – SCENE 3
THE BEDROOM IN DORIAN'S HOUSE

There is a bed and a small table with a trinket box on it containing a large, heavy looking key.

DORIAN and BASIL (Dressed as previous scene) enter from stage left.

Basil glances around, perplexed.

BASIL Where is it? You said the painting was here.

DORIAN I lied.

BASIL What?

DORIAN I don't want you to see the painting. It's in the attic. I've had a very secure iron door fitted to the stairs leading up there. It's locked and will remain that way.

BASIL Why on earth have you done that?

DORIAN If you saw it now, you'd want it locked away and never seen too. *(With a supressed laugh)* You certainly wouldn't want it hung up in the Hayward Gallery.

BASIL I don't understand.

DORIAN No, I don't suppose you do. *(He smiles and takes off his jacket)* Anyway, I haven't brought you up here on entirely false pretences. I promised that I was going to give you what you want and that's what I'm going to do.

Dorian pulls off his t-shirt.

BASIL What are you doing?

Dorian tosses his t-shirt onto the bed and begins to unbuckle his belt.

BASIL Dorian! *(Beat)* Stop it, you're embarrassing me.

DORIAN Do you really want me to stop?

BASIL *(Dropping his head)* No.

Dorian slowly develops a knowing smile.

Dorian moves over to the bed and sits. He then starts to take off his shoes and socks, then his trousers. As he does so...

DORIAN Why do you always look so damn miserable when things are going your way? I remember the first night we met, the triumphant opening of your exhibition – you had a face like an innocent man on trial being forced to plead guilty.

Dorian, now naked, gets to his feet and stands in front of Basil.

DORIAN Well, why?

BASIL *(Dropping his head)* I don't have an answer for you.

DORIAN I do – self-loathing.

Basil looks up and swallows. He then reaches out, his quivering hand about to touch Dorian's chest.

DORIAN I haven't said you can touch me, yet.

Basil's hand springs away.

DORIAN Get on your knees.

Basil frowns.

DORIAN I said, get on your knees!

Basil thinks for a moment then slowly gets down onto his knees and looks up at Dorian.

Dorian steps a little closer.

DORIAN Alright, you can touch me now.

Basil reaches up and touches Dorian's chest, caressing it. After a moment, he puts his arms around Dorian and holds him tight; pressing the side of his face into Dorian's body. Basil's eyes are closed, he breathes heavily through his mouth.

The lights dim a little.

Basil undresses. They kiss and touch each other as he does so.

They get into bed and embrace.

The lights dip to black out.

After a moment the lights go back up.

Basil lies on his back – he looks deep in thought.

Dorian sits up and examines Basil's expression for a moment.

DORIAN Happy now, Basil?

BASIL I think I am, yes.

DORIAN Yet you don't look very certain.

BASIL I can't stop thinking about something you said earlier. It's playing about in my mind.

DORIAN And what might that be?

BASIL You said, if I were to see the painting now, I'd want it shut away and never seen too. What did you mean?

DORIAN *(Sighs deeply)* So, in the midst of all this, you've decided to think about the painting and find some worry to drag yourself away from pleasure. You're incorrigible, Basil.

BASIL It was a very loaded statement. You must have meant something.

DORIAN Oh, I did. *(Sits up and examines Basil's face for a moment, then...)* You think your work has shocked people in the past, don't you?

BASIL Unfortunately, yes.

DORIAN Well, all that would be positively benign in comparison to what would happen if anyone was to see that thing up in the attic.

BASIL *(Sitting up)* You're saying that something's happened to the painting?

DORIAN *(Thinks, then...)* How long ago did you paint me?

BASIL Umm… it must be 12 years now.

DORIAN Have I aged a day since? Look at me! Have I aged a day since?

BASIL Not really, it is extraordinary.

DORIAN Well, the painting has.

BASIL *(Narrowing his eyes)* The painting has?

DORIAN The painting has aged in my place and it's more than just aged.

BASIL What?

DORIAN It's as if it's absorbed all of the contemptable things I've done. They're written into its features. And I'm responsible for some truly terrible things.

BASIL I really don't think I understand what you're saying.

Dorian gets out of bed and pulls on his trousers. As he does this...

DORIAN *(Casually)* It started with a few details in the eyes; I could see the cruelty in them, when I really looked. It grew from there. Now, the whole face has contorted into something quite terrifying. It's really hideous and exudes evil. Yes, I don't think that's too strong a word – evil.

Basil has been listening intently. As he does so, he pulls on his underwear and gets out of bed. He puts on his trousers.

DORIAN It's become the painting of a monster and I don't think it's finished yet. So you see, it must remain locked away.

BASIL You have the key, of course.

DORIAN Yes, here.

Dorian goes over to the table, opens the small trinket box and produces the key.

DORIAN You think I'm crazy, don't you? But you wouldn't if you saw it. If you saw it...

Dorian thinks for a moment as be plays with the key in his hands.

DORIAN Earlier, I said you couldn't see the picture, now I'm going to insist that you must.

BASIL I'd like to see it and what's happened to it.

DORIAN No you wouldn't. But you are going to.

Dorian heads for exit.

Basil quickly follows.

ACT 4 – SCENE 4
THE ATTIC IN DORIAN'S HOUSE

There is a thin haze in the air. The lights are low and gloomy.

There are a couple of boxes filled with bric-a-brac about the stage. One has a deadly looking knife inside.

The easel, with the painting, is to the front of stage right, facing away from the audience.

Basil and Dorian enter. Both are still bare chested. They each carry a torch. Beams of light shine ahead into the hazy gloom.

DORIAN *(Pointing his torch at the painting)* There.

BASIL *(Approaching the painting)* Good God!

DORIAN Look at it, look at it! Now do you understand? It's like some kind of divine phenomenon, don't you think?

BASIL What the hell have you done to it? *(A look of horror and worry on his face)* What's happened?

DORIAN You've never seen anything like it, have you? It's not so much a painting anymore, as a looking glass turned to my soul.

BASIL *(Turning to Dorian)* Dorian, I think you need to see a doctor.

DORIAN But I'm strong and healthy and young. It's only when I look at the painting, that I see all the ugliness I'm guilty of. The rest of the time, I'm completely impervious. It's like my guardian; do you see?

BASIL Yes, I think I do. *(Beat)* I never thought I'd hear myself say this, but you need to get rid of it, Dorian. The health of your mind is much more important than any painting. Even that one. *(Glancing back at the painting)* Especially that one.

DORIAN *(Grabbing Basil roughly by the upper arms)* But this poor, defenceless abomination is ours, Basil. You gave birth to it from my seed. I've nurtured it, whilst you stood by. How can you even suggest that I be parted from it?

BASIL *(Trying to pull away)* There are people that can help you, Dorian. *(Beat)* Now, let go of me, please.

Dorian releases Basil.

BASIL *(Gathering his thoughts – shaken)* I think I'd like to leave now.

Dorian marches over to one of the wooden boxes and grabs the knife from amongst the bric-a-brac.

DORIAN *(Brandishing the knife threateningly at Basil)* No. I don't want you to go.

BASIL Don't be absurd. Put that knife down.

Basil attempts to pass, but Dorian stands fast, blocking him. Basil tries to push him aside but Dorian grabs him and they struggle. In the scuffle, the knife jabs into Basil's side. Stunned, Basil staggers backwards. He presses his hand to the wound and looks down in disbelief at his blood soaked hand, then up at Dorian.

Dorian stands with the knife dripping with blood in his hand.

BASIL *(Confused, fighting the pain)* You've stabbed me.

Basil stumbles then collapses to the floor.

DORIAN Yes, I can see that. *(Beat)* I should feel bad, I suppose, but you know, I don't. If anything, I feel excited. *(Beat)* And I haven't actually felt excited in a long time. Not *really* excited.

BASIL *(Trying to sit up)* Dorian, you're not well. Something has gone very wrong with your mind. You need to get me an ambulance, *(Beat)* quickly.

Dorian steps forward so that he stands over Basil.

DORIAN *(Calmly)* Involve other people in this. *(Beat)* No. I don't think so.

BASIL *(Breathless)* You have to. I'm badly hurt, Dorian. I'll say nothing about you to the police. I'll tell the ambulance crew that the knife is mine and I fell on it. Tripped in the dark up here. That's what I'll say.

Dorian leans in and touches Basil's hair gently.

DORIAN I believe you would too. You've always had my wellbeing at heart. Haven't you?

BASIL Yes, yes, I have. *(Beat)* Dorian, you need to make that phone call now, *(Beat)* please.

DORIAN You're probably the best friend I will ever have. In so many ways, I owe you everything. And now, we're lovers too. You are unique in my life and so very special to me. And, ironically, it's because of all of that, that I need to know how this will feel.

BASIL *(Frightened)* How what will feel?

DORIAN I'm sorry, Basil but it's this.

Dorian takes Basil by the hair and pulls his head back. He lifts the knife looking deeply into his eyes. A look of total horror takes Basil's face as he stares up at Dorian. He's worked out what Dorian is about to do.

BASIL No!

Dorian slashes Basil's throat. Blood sprays out.

Dorian flings the knife aside. He cradles Basil in his arms; occasionally stroking his hair tenderly – an expression of tender deep affection and care on his face. This expression develops into one of sadness.

When Dorian is certain that Basil is dead, he gently
lowers the body to the floor. He then looks up, his face
is now blank, still and cold.

ACT 4 – SCENE 5
THE ATTIC IN DORIAN'S HOUSE

There is still a thin haze in the air. The lights at the very front of the stage go up, the rear of the stage is left in darkness.

Basil's body and the painting are obscured by the darkness – and they have both been covered up with sheets.

DORIAN (Now wearing a 1970s fashionable dressing gown) stands at the front of the stage. The 2 torches are near his feet, switched off.

ALAN (Wearing a 1970s brown wide-lapelled jacket, brown cords and a wide blue tie) enters and hurries toward Dorian.

DORIAN Thank God, you came.

ALAN Your message said it was a matter of life and death – of course I came. What's the matter, Dorian?

DORIAN Something terrible has happened. I don't know what to do, where to turn.

ALAN You can always turn to me, you know that. I'll do anything. Anything that'll help.

DORIAN That does make me feel better. If there's anyone who can get me out of this nightmare it's you, Alan. I do know that.

ALAN Right, tell me what's happened.

DORIAN OK. *(Beat)* In the attic of this house, there's a dead man. *(Beat)* Alan, I killed him.

ALAN What are you talking about?

DORIAN It was an accident. But people won't understand. I'll go to prison if you don't help me.

ALAN If this is some kind of strange game…

DORIAN It's not a game. Take this… *(He picks up the torches, turns them on and hands one to Alan)* Let me show you.

Dorian leads the way, Alan follows as…

The lights go up above the rest of the stage, but they are still low and gloomy. The haze still hangs in the air, picking up the torch beams.

Alan shines his torch around the room, then over to Basil's body covered with the sheet. There are two patches of blood seeping through the fabric – one near the neck, one near the belly.

ALAN Oh my God!

Dorian stands calmly to one side.

Alan dashes over, crouches and goes to pull the sheet off Basil's face.

DORIAN Before you look, there's something else I need to tell you. *(Takes a deep breath)* The man is Basil.

ALAN Basil!

Alan lifts the sheet and looks at the face. His hand springs up and covers his mouth.

ALAN Jesus Christ!

Alan covers Basil's face back up and recoils, springing to his feet.

DORIAN You've got to help me get rid of him. Get rid of him in such a way that nobody will ever find him.

ALAN *(Pacing and pushing his fingers through his*

hair) Got to think, got to think. Must try to think!

DORIAN Alan!

ALAN *(Stops pacing and turns to face Dorian)* That wasn't any accident. His throat's been cut.

Dorian grabs Alan's hand.

DORIAN He threatened me. There was a fight. It all happened so fast.

ALAN Threatened you. Basil. I don't believe that.

DORIAN It's true. It was terrible, Alan. I don't understand it either. That's why people can't know. I won't be capable of explaining. He was acting like a different person. An insane person.

ALAN *(Pulling his hand free)* Look, I don't know what the hell has gone on here, but I'm certainly not going to help you dispose of a dead body. Basil's dead body!

DORIAN *(Angry now)* You said you'd do anything!

ALAN I didn't know what you wanted then!

DORIAN You said anything! *(Beat)* You're disappointing me, Alan. Making extravagant promises you won't keep. Building my hopes up just to tread them mercilessly into the ground.

ALAN This is madness, Dorian. Why would you even think I'd help you with a thing like this? Why would you do a thing like this? Oh, God!

DORIAN I know you've dealt with dead things before and, more precisely, melting bodies in acids.

ALAN Animals! I've never destroyed a human body. And the human body of a person I knew and liked. *(Almost to himself)* You must have completely lost your mind!

Dorian grabs Alan by the arms.

DORIAN *(Pulling Alan close)* They'll put me in

prison for life. You'll never see me again. *(Softly)* We'll never be together, you'll never be able to kiss me, have me…

Dorian's lips have moved in very close to Alan's.

Alan almost seems mesmerised by Dorian for a moment, even tempted to kiss him, but then…

ALAN *(Pulling away)* None of that matters in comparison to me covering up a bloody murder.

DORIAN So you refuse.

ALAN Of course I refuse.

DORIAN Alan, you're forcing me to say things that I really don't want to say.

ALAN *(Deeply concerned)* Such as?

DORIAN If you don't help me, I'll tell everyone about us. Everything about us.

ALAN *(Sad, almost tearful)* You'd do that to me?

DORIAN Yes! Look at what you're perfectly prepared to turn round and do to me – just when I need you most. I see it as a very cowardly betrayal, Alan. But typical. Well, are you ready to have everyone know that you've been my secret lover?

ALAN It's been decriminalised for ten years. That kind of blackmail just won't work nowadays.

DORIAN Won't it? True, they won't put you in prison anymore. But have people's attitudes really changed that much? That's what I'd like to know.

ALAN Would you?

DORIAN Yes. For instance, it will be fascinating to see what the press do with it. What kind of tone they'll adopt. Things like that.

ALAN They'll be just as interested in you, once I've had my say.

DORIAN I expect they will. But you forget, I'll be in prison and past caring. Then again, say I was to get off, my reputation would thrive on another sex scandal. Can you say the same? Family audiences sitting down together for cosy evenings in front of the BBC. Giving the kids a boost for their science lessons at school – all very wholesome.

ALAN And you don't trade in the wholesome.

DORIAN Exactly. *(Beat)* You know, I can picture Life Lab being quietly dropped or the host side-lined until he's replaced. That would be a shame, don't you think?

Alan rubs the palm of his hand down his face.

ALAN I don't care. I'd rather lose all of it.

Dorian and Alan are standing very close now. Dorian takes hold of Alan by the upper arms and speaks almost tenderly to him...

DORIAN Would you? All of it? *(Beat)* How will your wife and little boy take the news? And not just the shock of when the information is fresh. No, I think it'll probably get more problematic for them in the years to come. At least now they have position and money to buffer the blow. But that will go, and they'll be left with only a washed-up, disgraced, has-been for a husband and father.

ALAN Shut up!

DORIAN It will be tough for them… and you. I worry about a relationship surviving in that sort of atmosphere, I really do. Honestly, Alan, I see nothing but ruination on every front if you persist in this reckless course of action.

ALAN *(Looking into Dorian's eyes lovingly)* God, I hate you. You're asking me to do something that will stain my soul, indelibly, forever.

DORIAN *(Indignant)* I think you should stop thinking about yourself and start considering your wife and child's feelings in all this. *(Beat)* Perhaps I'll also talk about how we frequently use drugs together too. Everyone is going to be so disenchanted.

Alan pulls away from Dorian and briskly paces the room again.

Dorian watches in silence.

Alan stops and bangs his fist against the wall in frustration. He turns to face Dorian.

ALAN I'll need a pen and paper. There'll be equipment and chemicals I'll need. I'll say they're for a feature I'm planning for the show. *(Beat)* Eventually, when I'm asked, I'll tell them I'm preparing a new, smaller scale version of the dissolving elephant I did in the 60s. This time with…I don't know…a dead cow or something. They'll hate the idea and it won't go ahead but it will explain the order of chemicals and equipment.

Dorian suddenly hugs Alan.

DORIAN How very cunning of you. I knew I'd turned to the right man when I was at my most desperate. You're such a good friend, Alan.

Alan pushes Dorian away.

ALAN *(Sad, weakened)* Friend? When this is over, I never want to see your face again. It disgusts me, you disgust me.

At this statement, Dorian's expression turns to one of almost childlike hurt and disappointment. He drops his head.

ACT 5 – SCENE 1
A NURSING HOME IN HAMPSTEAD
1999

The lights at the very front of the stage go up, the rear of the stage is left in darkness.

Upstage right, obscured by the darkness, is MAVIS wearing a black, lacy dressing gown, black turban and dark glasses. She is sitting in a wheelchair. Opposite her are two stools.

HARRY, now with grey hair and glasses, enters in the light at the front of the stage. He is wearing a rain coat over a smart 3-piece suit with a red silk tie and matching pocket square.

HETTY, now in her mid 30s, (wearing a parka jacket, jeans and top) follows him on. She has a camera on a strap round her neck and a fat leather bag.

They head for front and centre stage; as they walk…

HETTY You know, this is by far the most expensive nursing home in Hampstead… in London, probably.

HARRY It's sheer guilt, Hetty. You see, Mavis's family have no time for her. Knowing she's in geriatric luxury salves their conscience.

HETTY How long has she been here?

HARRY Let me see. *(Thinks)* They sent the old nuisance packing the day before Christmas Eve, '96 – almost 3 years now.

HETTY I see. *(Beat)* At least she's one of the ones that can be tracked down… and still alive.

They head up stage and the rest of the lights go up.

HARRY Mavis, this is the young lady I told you about… on the telephone… *(Glancing at Hetty)* yesterday.

MAVIS Good God, it's Sybil Vane.

HARRY No, this is Hetty, Sybil's daughter.

MAVIS Hetty, oh. *(She takes hold of both of Hetty's hands and looks deeply into her eyes)* The last time I saw you, you were still in your pushchair – now look at me. *(She pats the arms of the wheelchair)*

HARRY *(Sitting down on a stool)* Hetty's writing a book. I did explain.

MAVIS *(Looking Hetty up and down)* Writing a book?

Hetty sits on a stool too. She plonks her bag on the floor next to her.

HETTY Yes. About my mother… and the people she knew. I'm also getting some photographs. *(She holds up her camera)* May I?

MAVIS *(Quickly adjusts her turban and smiles broadly)* Of course.

FLASH – Hetty takes a photograph. She then gets out a note pad and pen

HETTY One person I wanted to ask the two of you about is the artist Basil Hallward and what you think happened to him?

MAVIS Basil Hallward. *(Beat)* Some say he's dead, but I suspect different. And I'll tell you why – he's…

HARRY *(Interrupting)* Yes, yes, there've been reported sightings of Basil over the years. But are these people any more reliable than all those who say they've caught a glimpse of Lord Lucan.

MAVIS I think they are. I think Basil is living it up in Morocco under an assumed name and an artfully altered appearance. A well-tended moustache would do the trick. And he'd have to wear dark glasses with all that sunshine. He's been spotted there more than once.

HARRY He's been spotted in Thailand just as often. Not to mention Goa.

MAVIS Wherever he is, it was all a stunt. Everyone knew he'd shrivelled up as an artist. He'd been putting it about that he was going off travelling the world. Searching for inspiration... Searching for inspiration my eye. He was readying his vanishing act.

HARRY Ridiculous.

MAVIS Not so ridiculous when you notice the way his paintings became more and more valuable after his disappearance. An original Basil Hallward became almost priceless. He's in some sunny paradise counting the cash.

HARRY I'd be inclined to give that theory house room, if I didn't know Basil. Not the sort of thing he'd be capable of.

MAVIS Perhaps you put him up to it, Harry.

Harry and Mavis look at each other and chuckle.

Hetty studies them for a moment, then...

HETTY The last sighting of Basil that can actually be confirmed is rather interesting, I think. *(Glances at her note pad)* 21st of September, 1977. A cab driver collected him from a meeting at the Hayward Gallery on the South Bank and dropped him at Dorian Gray's house near Regent's Park. This was at approximately 8pm. Do either of you think Dorian saw Basil that evening?

HARRY *(Emphatically)* No, Dorian was out and didn't get back 'til late.

HETTY You seem very certain.

HARRY I am certain. It's a night I've had to talk about many times. You see, Dorian was with me the entire time. We went to a club called Rags and didn't part company until well after midnight.

HETTY *(Crossing something out in her note pad)* Yes, nobody would've hung around in the street, waiting for over 4 hours – Basil would've needed to be obsessed with Dorian to do a thing like that.

HARRY *(Distracted)* Exactly. Basil would have simply found nobody at home and just took himself off. Where he ended up, I fear we'll never know.

MAVIS Morocco! And I do recall once overhearing Joe Orton telling him all about the many delights of Marrakech. *(She winks at Hetty)*

HETTY If he did suddenly go off on a trip abroad, wouldn't that seem very odd? I mean, with a major exhibition of his work about to open.

HARRY Not really. He wouldn't have particularly wanted to attend any opening night dos or anything like that. He hated that sort of fuss. Anyway, all the plans for the exhibition were in place.

MAVIS Apart from securing what would've been the centrepiece – The Picture of Dorian Gray.

HETTY *(Thoughtfully)* Yes, apart from that. Which takes me right back to Dorian.

Harry folds his arms and looks suspiciously at Hetty.

HARRY *(Adopting a charming smile)* With Basil gone missing, Dorian was just too distraught to permit it. They were very, very close, you see, Hetty. *(Beat)* And he'd always promised your mother that it would never go on public display – it was just for them.

HETTY *(With slight sarcasm)* How romantic of him. *(Beat)* Umm. *(To Mavis)* And of course, you knew my mother quite well.

MAVIS Oh, yes. We were great friends. She simply

91

loved the book I wrote about her.

HETTY *(With incredulity)* She liked it?

MAVIS Yes, yes. I think she saw it as the tough love it was intended to be; a therapeutic kindness, from me to her. *(Mavis seems lost in a happy memory for a moment, then...)* You know, I consider her to be one of the most important tragic icons of the 60s... *(Beat)* after Monroe, of course... *(Beat)* and Kennedy.

Harry looks across at Hetty and raises his eyebrows.

Hetty tries to control the look of disbelief on her face and flicks though her note pad.

HETTY *(As she does so, collecting her thoughts)* OK... and then there's this other man that strikes me as important. Alan Campbell, he used to be on the telly.

HARRY Oh, poor Alan. He always seemed such a straight laced sort of chap, then he went completely off the rails for no apparent reason.

Hetty makes a note.

MAVIS Yes, Alan. If ever there was a Jekyll and Hyde it was Alan Campbell. Always looked as if butter wouldn't melt, but I had my eye on him from the start. *(Chuckles)* Drink, drugs, illicit sex, sacked from the BBC, divorce and obscurity. It was my front page that first exposed his secret vices. It shocked the nation.

HARRY He seemed to change overnight and become haunted by something; no idea what. I remember meeting him for a drink just before the story broke. He'd gone downhill fast. I could tell he was trying to escape some demon. Some demon inside his head. *(Shaking his head)* But that was over twenty years ago. God knows where he is today.

HETTY Umm, another dead end. *(Turns a page in her note pad)* Getting back to Dorian Gray, my stepfather. He was also a friend?

MAVIS I knew him. *(Beat)* Well, I say I knew him.

But who can say they ever truly knew Dorian. Perhaps you, Harry?

Harry just smiles.

MAVIS *(To Hetty)* Do you have any fond memories, dear?

HETTY Me? No. I use the word 'stepfather', but the closest I've ever got is magazine articles, record covers and photos in the press. He did manage my trust fund until I was 18. He was very fair, so I understand, but there was no contact.

MAVIS Just as well, love. He'd have been no father to a child. His life's been one scandal after another. *(Beat)* There'd have been money though. Pots of money. We all know how his career went stratospheric in the early 80s. Platinum albums, stadiums, the lot. Some say he lost his artistic integrity, but I loved his music then.

HARRY Did you?

MAVIS Yes. You could really dance to it and it worked ever so well on that advert for Fanta. *(Beat)* But he was already becoming more and more of a recluse. Then, suddenly, he cut everyone off. Ruthless, he was.

HETTY *(Writing in the pad)* Yep, not been seen in public for over a decade.

HARRY Even I haven't seen hide nor hair of him since the late 80s and we'd been inseparable once.

MAVIS I know. I don't suppose you were expecting him to turn round and piss all over your dinner like that, Harry.

Harry throws Mavis an irritated, sideways glance.

Mavis grins back.

MAVIS I bet you still get your ten percent, though.

HARRY I do.

HETTY *(Bitterly)* I'd hoped the great Dorian Gray would grant me an audience to help me with this, all things considered. But no. I'd have had more luck trying to pop round to see Howard Hughes.

HARRY I ran into his son the other day. The lad's 21– looks just like his father. I mean, he looks just like Dorian did in the 60s. You strongly resemble your mother, but this is nothing short of uncanny.

MAVIS I didn't know he had a son.

HARRY You're slipping in your old age, Mavis. It wasn't public knowledge whilst the boy was growing up, but he materialised fully formed a couple of years ago. One of the few things we've had out of Dorian this decade was that open letter to the press confirming the whole business.

MAVIS Juicy, very juicy. There's nothing like a secret love child to stir things up.

HETTY Are you telling me his son is in London?

HARRY Yes, staying at your mother's old house, the one on Regent's Park. Well, Dorian's house.

MAVIS I thought that place had been closed up for years. Gone to rack and ruin, I'd expect.

HARRY Closed up and in moth balls, yet rigorously maintained, so I understand.

HETTY *(Thoughtfully, tapping her pen on her pad)* So, Dorian's son is living in that house, is he? *(Beat)* Harry, I'll need to speak to him next. *(Standing and putting away her pad and pen in her bag)* Could you introduce me?

HARRY *(Also standing)* Is an introduction necessary? He is a sort of brother.

HETTY I don't think I could ever think of him as a brother. I really would appreciate it.

HARRY Then I shall.

HETTY *(To Mavis)* Thank you for your time, Mrs Ruxton.

MAVIS Harry…?

HARRY *(Turing back)* Yes, Mavis.

MAVIS You will come and visit me again soon, won't you? Nobody tells me all about what's going on anymore. You always did know the best gossip. I get ever so bored… *(Beat)* bored and lonely.

ACT 5 – SCENE 2
THE ROMILLY CLUB
(FORMERLY THE BLUE TURTLE) IN SOHO

The easel is to the rear of stage right and is set with a large 'Romilly Club' sign.

There is the sound of the gentle chatter of a fashionable London club. 90s Brit Pop plays in the background. A thin, smoky haze hangs in the air.

HETTY and HARRY (Dressed as the previous scene but without the coats) are sitting on stools at a small club table. There is an amber table lamp at the centre, plus an open bottle of white wine in a wine cooler and 3 glasses.

DORIAN (now in his mid 50s but passing as his own 21 year old son) sits between them. He is dressed in jeans, a collarless shirt and a khaki jacket.

Dorian pours each of them a glass of wine; as he does so…

DORIAN I really can't tell you that much, I'm afraid. I haven't got to know my father very well, yet. I was brought up by my mother, you see. He met her in late 77, early 78. Anyway, let's just say that their relationship was brief.

Hetty puts her notepad and pen down on the table.

HETTY Umm. *(Beat)* I'd be very interested in visiting the Regent's Park house and seeing Basil Hallward's painting, The Picture of Dorian Gray.

DORIAN Why?

HETTY Well, for one thing, I'd like to photograph you with the famous portrait of your father. The two of you together, with him the same age as you are now.

DORIAN I suppose that would be interesting.

HETTY They say the resemblance is more than striking.

DORIAN Yes, that's what they say. But it will be impossible for you to see the painting, sorry.

Harry takes a cigarette from a case and lights it. He looks back and forth between Dorian and Hetty with subtle interest as they speak.

HETTY I understood it was still at the house.

DORIAN That's right, it's in the attic room, but there's a metal door with a rather strong lock. The thing was fitted back in the 70s… I'm told. I've never been in there; don't have the key.

HETTY *(Narrowing her eyes)* That seems like a rather unusual arrangement. One room locked up like that for decades… all a bit Jane Eyre, don't you think?

DORIAN *(Seemingly amused)* When you put it like that, I suppose so.

HARRY *(With a mischievous smile)* Dorian will have a key, surely.

DORIAN *(A little thrown)* Yes, Dad will have the key, but I don't really know where he is right now or how to contact him.

HARRY You two don't see much of each other then. I'd have thought he'd have wanted to make up for all those lost years.

DORIAN I'll probably spend Christmas with him… or maybe we'll see in the year 2000 together.

HARRY *(Nodding)* How heart-warming. I for one

would love to see the two of you pull a Christmas cracker together or simply joining hands to sing a chorus or two of 'Auld Lang Syne'.

HETTY *(Thoughtfully)* Either way, it'll be too late for my book.

DORIAN That is a pity. But it's out of my hands. I do apologise.

HETTY *(Thinking)* Not your fault, I can see that.

DORIAN Anyway, I'm certain Harry here can tell you about enough scandal from back then to fill half a dozen books.

Harry chuckles to himself.

Hetty puts her note pad and pen away in her bag.

HETTY I'm sorry to have wasted your time.

DORIAN Not at all, it's been a pleasure to meet you at last. Though I can't help but say, it feels as if I've known you for years.

HETTY *(With a small frown)* Really?

DORIAN Yes. I'm quite a fan. I've read all your books. Every one of them. I think they're brilliant. So very insightful.

HARRY I couldn't agree more. Her research always seems to uncover some fascinating twist; doesn't it?

HETTY *(With a small smile)* You're both too kind.

DORIAN No, your work is outstanding. Your mother would have been very proud... I would have thought.

Hetty studies Dorian's face for a moment, then...

HETTY I really wanted to get some photos of you at the Regent's Park house – painting or no painting. Would that be OK?

HARRY *(Staring at Dorian)* Now that does sound doable. Wouldn't you say?

DORIAN Umm… We could certainly arrange that… I suppose.

HETTY Shall we say, tomorrow afternoon, about 4ish?

HARRY No sense hanging about, is there?

DORIAN Umm…alright, yes. *(Beat)* I'll look forward to it.

HETTY It's a date then. *(Standing)* Goodbye, for now, Mr Gray.

DORIAN *(With a small smile)* Ciao.

Hetty makes for the exit stage left.

Harry hasn't moved, he remains seated.

HARRY *(Calling after her)* I'll catch you up, Hetty.

HETTY *(Turning back)* Sure. I need to get a few pictures of the outside of the building, anyway. This place used to be the notorious Blue Turtle.

HARRY Did it really? *(Softly)* Fancy that.

Dorian takes a cigarette case and lighter from his pocket.

Harry turns back to Dorian and leans in.

HARRY It's you, isn't it?

DORIAN I don't understand. What?

HARRY You can't kid me, Dorian. What have you done to yourself. It's incredible.

Dorian smiles and holds Harry's gaze for a second. He then lights a cigarette.

DORIAN *(Blows smoke from the corner of his mouth, then…)* Oh, Harry, of all the people still left, naturally, you'd be the one who'd see straight through me.

HARRY There can be nothing natural about this.

DORIAN We can't talk here. *(Glances round)* Come to my house tomorrow evening. Come alone. I'll explain everything then.

HARRY *(Narrowing his eyes, thoughtful)* Until tomorrow then.

Harry stands and starts to leave, but he stops and turns back.

HARRY A word of caution concerning the lovely Miss Vane. She says this book of hers is about Sybil, but I've noticed that her questions all orbit the dark star of Dorian Gray. *(Harry then smiles broadly)* Just a little something for you to mull over.

ACT 5 – SCENE 3
ARCHER STREET
IN SOHO

It is dark and shadowy with a thin haze in the air. There is a brighter patch of light from a spot – the light from the street lamp. The sound of the city and Soho hums – cars, people.

ALAN (Now in his late 50s, dressed in a worn Crombie overcoat and scarf) stands centre upstage. He looks old beyond his years – sallow, grey and ill.

DORIAN (Dressed as the previous scene) enters from stage left and walks across the stage. He is about to pass Alan when…

ALAN *(Putting an unlit cigarette into his mouth)* Got a light?

DORIAN *(Stopping)* Yes. Here you go.

Dorian takes out a lighter, lights it and raises it to Alan's cigarette. The flame glows between the two men's faces.

ALAN *(Suddenly dropping his cigarette and grabbing Dorian's wrist)* I knew it was you, I knew it was you from the moment I saw you.

Alan punches Dorian in the guts.

Dorian flies backwards landing on the ground.

Alan pulls out a gun, stands over Dorian and presses it to his forehead.

ALAN *(Grinning, manic, nodding)* I'm going to kill you now, blow your evil fucking brains out. Ordinary people aren't safe with a fucking monster like you allowed to roam the streets.

DORIAN What?

ALAN *(Still grinning, manic, nodding)* Get ready to have that face blasted into bloody oblivion, you fucking bastard. It's what you deserve. It's what you've deserved for a long time. I'll be doing society an important service.

DORIAN Who the hell do you think I am?

ALAN Dorian Gray – I'd know you anywhere. I saw you earlier today, on Old Compton Street. I've been following you ever since. Watching you. Having the audacity to walk about the place, acting like a normal, harmless man.

DORIAN You think you recognise me.

ALAN *(Angry)* Of course I recognised you! *(Suddenly calm)* You haven't changed a bit.

DORIAN There…there, you said it. You said it.

ALAN What?

DORIAN This man, this man Dorian Gray. How old would he be?

ALAN Mid-fifties, by now.

DORIAN Get me under that street lamp and look at me. Look at my face.

ALAN *(Angry again)* I know well enough what you look like.

DORIAN *(Forcefully)* No, you don't. You need to look at me properly and think. Get me under that lamp. Now!

Alan grabs Dorian by the neck and drags him across the stage. He holds him down under the spot of light.

DORIAN *(Catching his breath)* Now can you see.

ALAN *(Shaken)* Yes. Yes, I can.

DORIAN How old would you say I am?

ALAN *(Sad)* Twenty, perhaps twenty one.

DORIAN Exactly.

Alan lowers the gun

ALAN *(Suddenly and alarmingly jovial and friendly, but maintaining a firm grip on Dorian)* I was going to kill you. I intended to do it. I really was. Another innocent victim of that man. Another innocent victim of that man and me.

DORIAN *(Taking out his wallet)* Let me give you some money, you look as if you…

ALAN *(Not really listening to Dorian)* But, this would've been all my doing. *(Nods)* That's what I've become, you see – a drunk and a drug addict lurking in the shadows at night. *(Strokes Dorian's face with gun)* So twisted and obsessed I'm ready to kill some random, blameless boy on the streets. I don't know what's real anymore. I need to take responsibility for that much.

Alan lets go and gently strokes Dorian's face.

ALAN You have lovely skin, do you know that?
(Beat) I expect you do.

DORIAN You need help.

ALAN *(Laughs)* I contaminate everything I touch.

Alan turns the gun on himself and puts the barrel under his chin.

DORIAN No, don't.

Dorian grabs Alan's hands and tries to pull the gun away. He manages to get it ways from Alan's head, but they continue to struggle.

DORIAN Alan, don't please!

103

On the use of his name, Alan's eyes widen.

ALAN You do know me! My God, it is you! My Dorian.

Dorian reacts with horror to Alan's recognition of him. He lets go of Alan's hand and backs away.

DORIAN No, I'm not! As you said – you don't know what's real.

Alan nods slowly with a broad smile on his face.

ALAN Umm. *(Nods)* Yes, that is true *(Beat)* and it's probably for the best, all things considered.

DORIAN *(Coldly)* Perhaps you'd be better off dead.

Alan nods at Dorian. He presses the gun to his temple and puts his finger back on the trigger.

ALAN *(With a sad, resigning smile, nodding)* That's what I thought. *(Beat)* Anyway, bye, bye, Dorian. I'm so pleased we've had this opportunity to catch up.

BANG! The gun goes off.

Alan's body dops to the ground.

Dorian stands over the body for a moment, he looks down with a sorrowful expression.

There is suddenly the distinct sound of a police siren.

Dorian looks around frantically. He then grabs the gun and then runs off.

ACT 5 – SCENE 4
THE LIVING ROOM
DORIAN'S HOUSE

DORIAN (Dressed as the previous scene but without the jacket) stands to stage left.

HETTY (Wearing jeans and top) Has her camera in hand begins photographing him. The camera flashes. Flash. Flash. Flash!

Her bag sits open on a small table along with her note pad and pen.

90s style Trip Hop music plays softly.

HETTY I think these are going to look great. Perhaps, when they're published, they'll do for you what the painting did for your father.

DORIAN *(Amused)* I very much doubt that.

Hetty takes another photo. Flash!

HETTY Just a moment.

Hetty goes over to Dorian. She unbuttons his shirt. Then lets her hand drift down his exposed chest.

HETTY *(Stepping back, looking Dorian up and down)* That's even better.

They exchange a smile, then Hetty takes a few more photos. Flash. Flash!

HETTY So, this is the room where the painting used to hang. *(Gestures towards the front of stage right)* It was over there? Yes?

DORIAN Possibly, I really don't know.

HETTY Yes, that's where it was *(Glancing around)* Harry told me. He described everything vividly.

DORIAN Do you remember anything of this house?

HETTY Nothing. Nothing at all. I was just a baby the last time I was here. Back in the days before Dorian Gray. I never did get to live here.

DORIAN Yes, the custody… I'm certain they tried very hard.

HETTY Not hard enough. *(Pointing at where the painting used to be)* Can you go and stand over there?

Dorian walks over to the front of stage right and turns back to face Hetty.

Hetty points the camera and focuses. Flash! Flash!

HETTY I think I'd like some photos of you in another part of the house next. *(Beat)* Why don't you show me where your bedroom is?

DORIAN My bedroom?

Hetty puts the camera down on the table and walks over to Dorian. They stand very close indeed, holding eye contact. After a few seconds, Hetty moves in and kisses Dorian on the mouth. This becomes a long, lingering kiss.

DORIAN *(Pulling away)* Look, Hetty. *(Beat)* I… I have an appointment. Harry will be here soon.

HETTY That is disappointing.

DORIAN True, but necessary. I think you should leave before he gets here.

HETTY *(Taken aback)* Leave? *(Beat)* But I'd like to see Harry myself.

Dorian rebuttons his shirt.

DORIAN He and I have something private to discuss.

I'm going to need to be alone with him. You really must go now.

HETTY Then I'll go. *(Beat)* Another time then?

DORIAN I don't think so.

Hetty goes over to the table and hurriedly starts to put her camera, pad and pen into her bag, clearly irritated and confused.

Dorian watches her for a moment, then…

DORIAN Good luck with the book. I hope it sells like cold pop in a heatwave.

HETTY *(Slinging the bag over her shoulder)* That's a funny way of putting it.

DORIAN Yes, I've always thought so. Goodbye, Hetty.

HETTY Look, *(Attempting a smile)* goodbyes always sound so final. Why don't we keep in touch and see what happens?

DORIAN Not a good idea. I'm leaving London soon. Don't know where I'm going yet. Best we keep this as a goodbye.

HETTY *(Examines Dorian's expression for a moment then…)* Did you work out that I was only using you? Getting close in an attempt to get to Dorian?

DORIAN If that's truly what you had in mind, you'll never know how effective that tactic could have been. *(Kindly)* Anyway, I know the face of a cynical, mercenary bastard when I see one and I'm not looking at one now.

HETTY *(Narrowing her eyes)* Dorian's always thrived on publicity, any publicity. But the more I dig, the more I'm certain that there's something hidden that even he doesn't want out there.

DORIAN *(Suddenly, the kindness is gone. Cold)* Good luck with that one. As I say, goodbye, Hetty.

HETTY *(She shrugs)* You're too young for me anyway.

Hetty quickly exits.

Dorian stands centre stage and watches her go.

ACT 5 – SCENE 5
THE ATTIC IN DORIAN'S HOUSE

A thin haze hangs in the air. The lights are low and gloomy.

There are a couple of boxes filled with bric-a-brac about the stage. One sits on a small table and contains the metronome and an old pamphlet from Basil's 1965 exhibition. The easel with the painting is to the front of stage right, facing away from the audience. There is a bench towards the rear of the stage.

HARRY (Wearing his 3-piece suit with a red silk tie and matching pocket square) and DORIAN (Costume as previous scene) are gazing at the painting. They each hold a torch, the beams glow in the haze.

HARRY *(Eyes fixed on the painting)* It's utterly extraordinary. *(Beat)* I can honestly say, I've never seen anything like it in my life.

DORIAN I should have told you all about it from the start. I should have always known if anyone would understand, it's you.

HARRY Well, 'understand' might be stretching it… to say the least. *(Turns to Dorian)* But I do believe, which is always the more important of the two.

They both go to sit and place their torches on the bench.

DORIAN *(As he goes, amused)* Oh, I've missed you, Harry. *(More serious and almost to himself)* I've missed you more than I can say.

HARRY *(Flippantly)* I'm certain there've been compensations.

DORIAN Of a sort… perhaps.

Harry takes a hipflask from his pocket and pours some whisky into a small chrome cup. He hands it to Dorian, but without letting go…

HARRY I saw the lovely Hetty leaving as I arrived. She seemed more than a little distracted. I do hope you haven't confided in her, have you?

DORIAN No. I told her to go. I won't see her again.

Harry releases the cup.

HARRY You didn't desire her?

Harry takes a swig from the flask.

DORIAN Oh, I wanted her, but I knew it would be wrong. That ultimately, I'd cause more pain. And I'm tired of causing pain. So very tired.

HARRY How dreary. The thought of you two together is delicious, on so many levels.

DORIAN Don't, Harry. I'm searching for absolution. If Dorian couldn't be good, perhaps his son can be.

HARRY But you're not your own son, Dorian. Let's not confuse this matter any further.

DORIAN *(Standing)* Look at me! What choice is there? I have to show the world something. Perhaps I can be something better.

HARRY *(Standing)* Has posing as your own son proven good for your soul so far?

DORIAN Not in the slightest. *(Beat)* In fact, it's already led to more evil. My soul's not with me, you see; *(Flicking his hand at the painting)* it's trapped in The Picture of Dorian Gray.

HARRY Don't be so bloody melodramatic.

DORIAN If any situation called for melodrama, Harry, surely it's this one.

HARRY *(Touching Dorian's chest)* I'm certain your soul resides where it always has.

DORIAN *(Looking into Harry's eyes)* There was a time when my only fear was that I'd end up in hell. Silly, isn't it? Now I've reached the conclusion that this is hell and that I've been here for a long time.

HARRY *(Lightly)* That kind of damnation seems a tad severe for any crimes you might have committed.

DORIAN You think so? *(Takes a slug of whisky)* What if I were to tell you that I murdered Basil and that his is not the only blood on my hands?

HARRY *(Narrowing his eyes)* What? Like you once told me you'd murdered Sybil?

DORIAN No, actual murder, *(Beat)* with a knife.

Harry turns away from Dorian and carefully screws the lid back onto his hipflask – thinking.

HARRY *(Firmly)* Then I wouldn't believe you and I hope nobody else would either.

DORIAN Alan Campbell, would.

HARRY What?

DORIAN Alan Campbell, would. *(Beat)* I forced him to help me dispose of the body, you see. *(Beat)* Thanks to that, he became quite mentally unstable. You must have noticed the change in him back then – of course you did. *(Beat)* I ran into him yesterday; can you believe it? Right on the streets of Soho.

HARRY *(Worried)* Did he work out who you really are?

DORIAN Oh, he knew me.

HARRY *(Alarmed, yet controlled)* Jesus Christ, this could turn out to be one monumental bloody problem.

DORIAN *(Calm)* Don't worry, he won't be telling anyone. *(Beat)* He killed himself you see; blew his brains out, right in front of me. He used this gun.

Dorian goes into his inside pocket and takes out the gun. It seems to be aimed at Harry now. A look of fear flashes across Harry's face.

Dorian looks Harry in the eye and notices his supressed panic, but he then just smiles and hands Harry the gun.

HARRY *(Breathes a sigh of relief and looks down at the gun in his hand)* That was helpful of him. *(Beat)* But then again, *(Looks back up at Dorian)* Alan always was an obliging sort of chap.

Harry walks to the small table and places the gun down next to the bric-a-brac box. He then stands looking down at the gun. As he does this...

HARRY Dorian, there's the attractively dangerous on the one hand, but there's the repellently ugly on the other. The public demands that you don't cross that line. Murder is hideously unappealing and can never be part of your story. *(Turning back to Dorian)* Never!

DORIAN Stories need an ending, Harry.

Harry walks back to Dorian. They are now standing quite close, facing each other.

HARRY That's very true and I suspect we've reached that juncture with you. *(Beat)* But your image will go on. It can strengthen and grow without you.

DORIAN Is that the best I can hope for?

HARRY Living legends have a sell-by date. There comes a point when you need to accept that your most valuable asset is your past.

DORIAN So it's my past that's of value now. Once upon a time you told me it was only my youth.

HARRY You might look young, Dorian, but you're

not. For you, the present and the future are becoming quite problematic. They have the potential to make things so untidy. Your worst crime now would be to vandalise your carefully constructed public image. Think about that image and your musical legacy. Superb commodities, held in time, ready to be exploited for decades to come – perhaps forever. Who can say what lustrous opportunities the new century will bring?

DORIAN *(Thinks for a beat then...)* Yes, I can see it – the Dorian Gray we've created reaching out into the future – never changing, never sullied. That way, perhaps, it won't have been so futile after all. *(With sad resignation)* I think I know what I need to do.

HARRY *(With sorrow)* I'm very glad to hear it.

Harry looks back over to the gun on the table, then back at Dorian.

HARRY I'm going now. We won't see each other again. Will we?

DORIAN *(Touching Harry on the arm)* You once said I'd never have to be without you.

HARRY Dorian Gray will always have me. I'll take care of everything.

They embrace, warmly but with sadness in their eyes.

DORIAN Goodbye, Harry.

HARRY Goodbye, Dorian.

They let go of each other and Harry exits.

Dorian watches him go, deep in thought.

Dorian goes over to the table and picks up the gun.

He notices something in the bric-a-brac box. He puts down the gun and, with a sorrowful expression, fishes out an old pamphlet from Basil's 1965 exhibition; he looks at it for a moment.

He then goes back into the box and takes out the metronome. He opens the door and sets the arm in motion. He now looks close to tears.

Tick, tick, tick, tick...

Dorian picks up the gun.

He then goes over to the bench and sits down. He looks at the Picture of Dorian Gray then down at the gun in his hand. After a moment of contemplation, he looks up and out over the audience. The sorrow has gone from his face. He breathes in deeply and starts to develop a smile.

The lights fade slowly to blackout.

THE END.

FRANZ KAFKA
APPARATUS

A PLAY BY ROSS DINWIDDY

Printed in Great Britain
by Amazon